Bird Lyrics

The Real Re-Imagined for Colorists

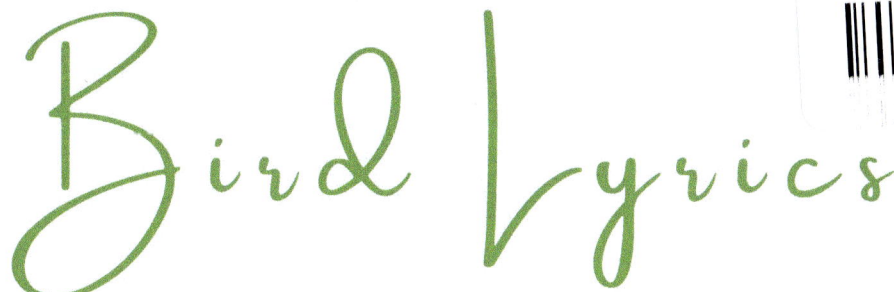

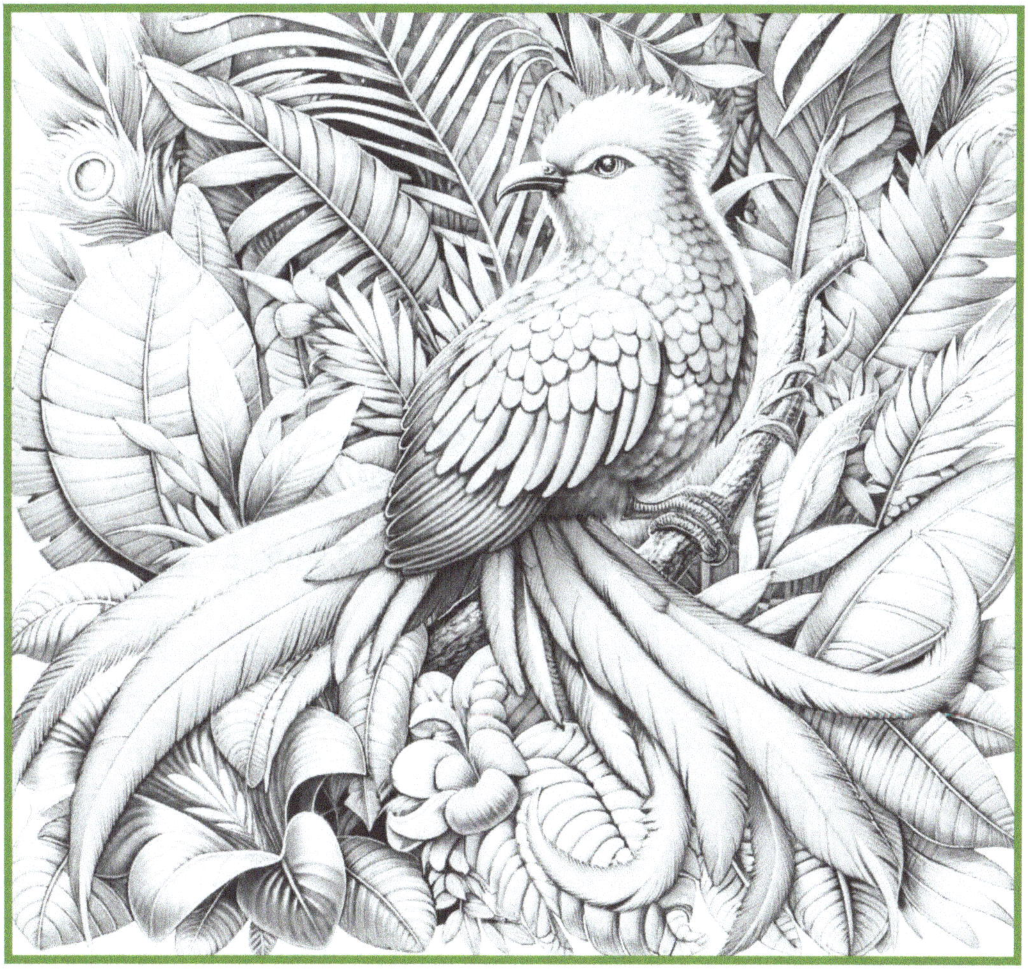

Bird Lyrics

This coloring book presents real birds in a creative and imaginative way, reimagining them with lyrical charm. Each page unveils a unique and delightful interpretation of different birds, turning feathers into whimsical visual poetry and melodies. From the graceful hummingbird to the majestic Giant Ibis, every bird is depicted with a touch of magic and charm. Immerse yourself in the intricate designs as you color, letting your imagination take flight with these captivating creatures. Allow yourself to be inspired by the natural melodies as you bring vibrant life to these beautiful birds.

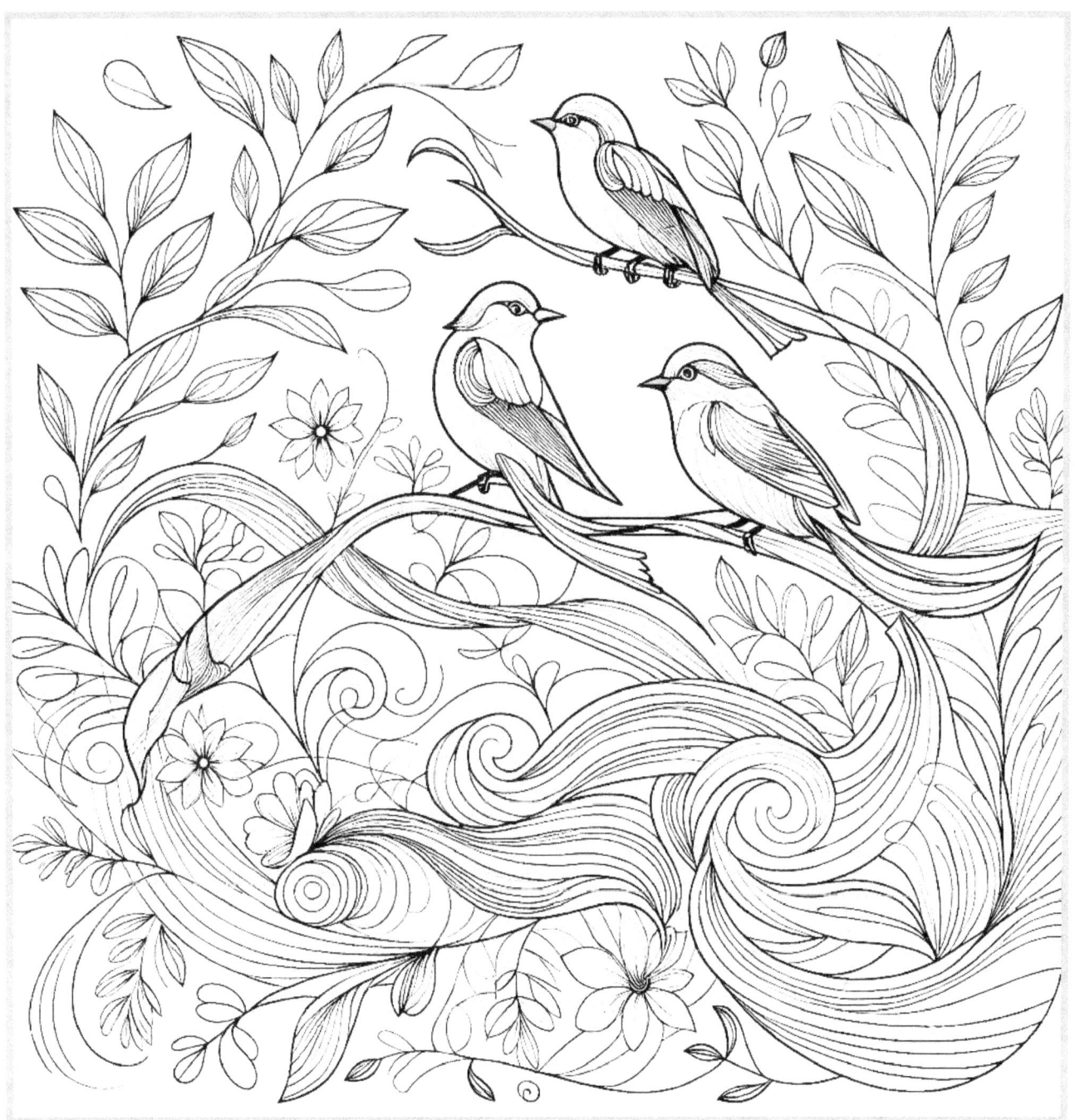

Blue-eyed Ground-Dove

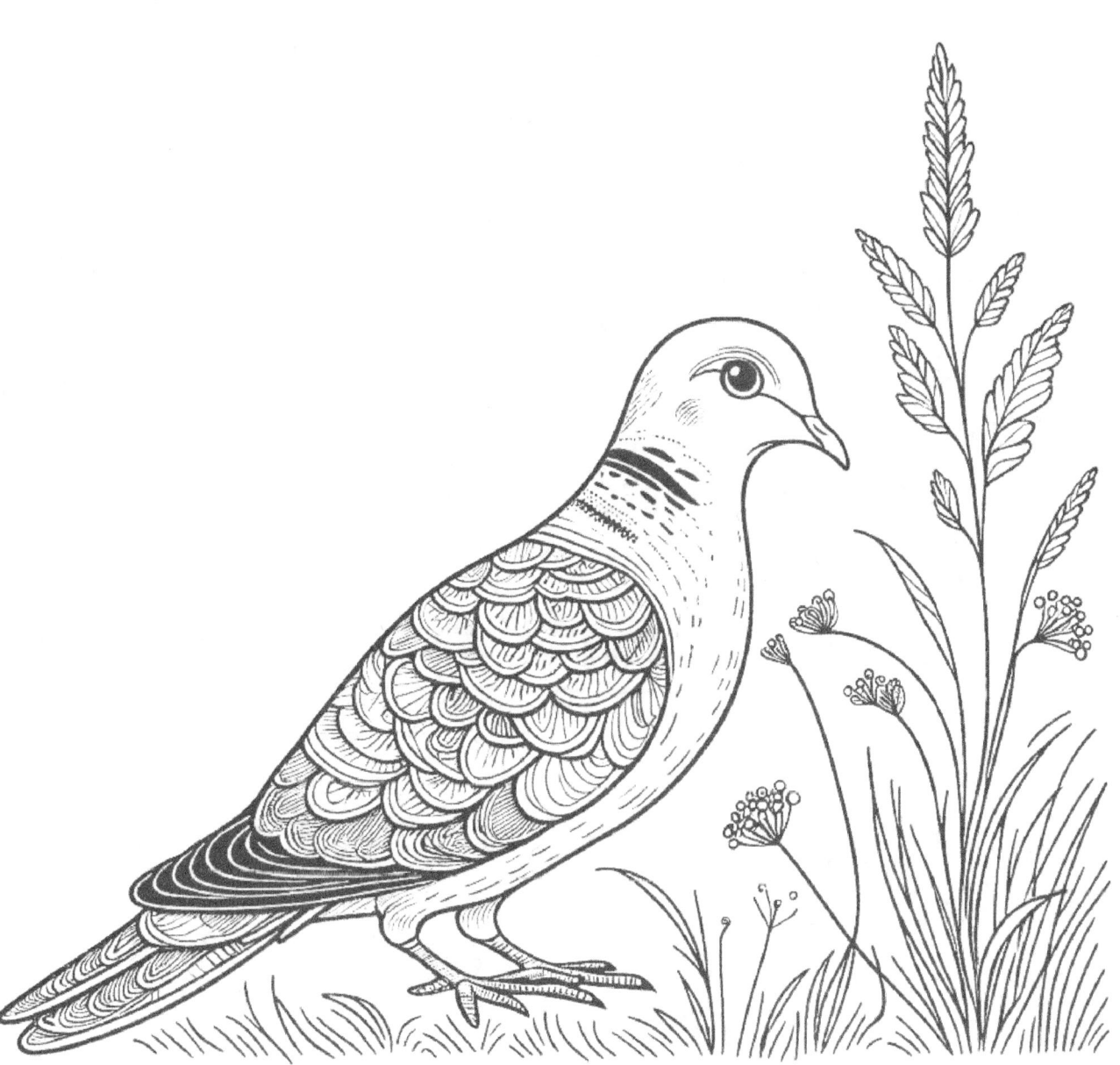

Painted Bunting

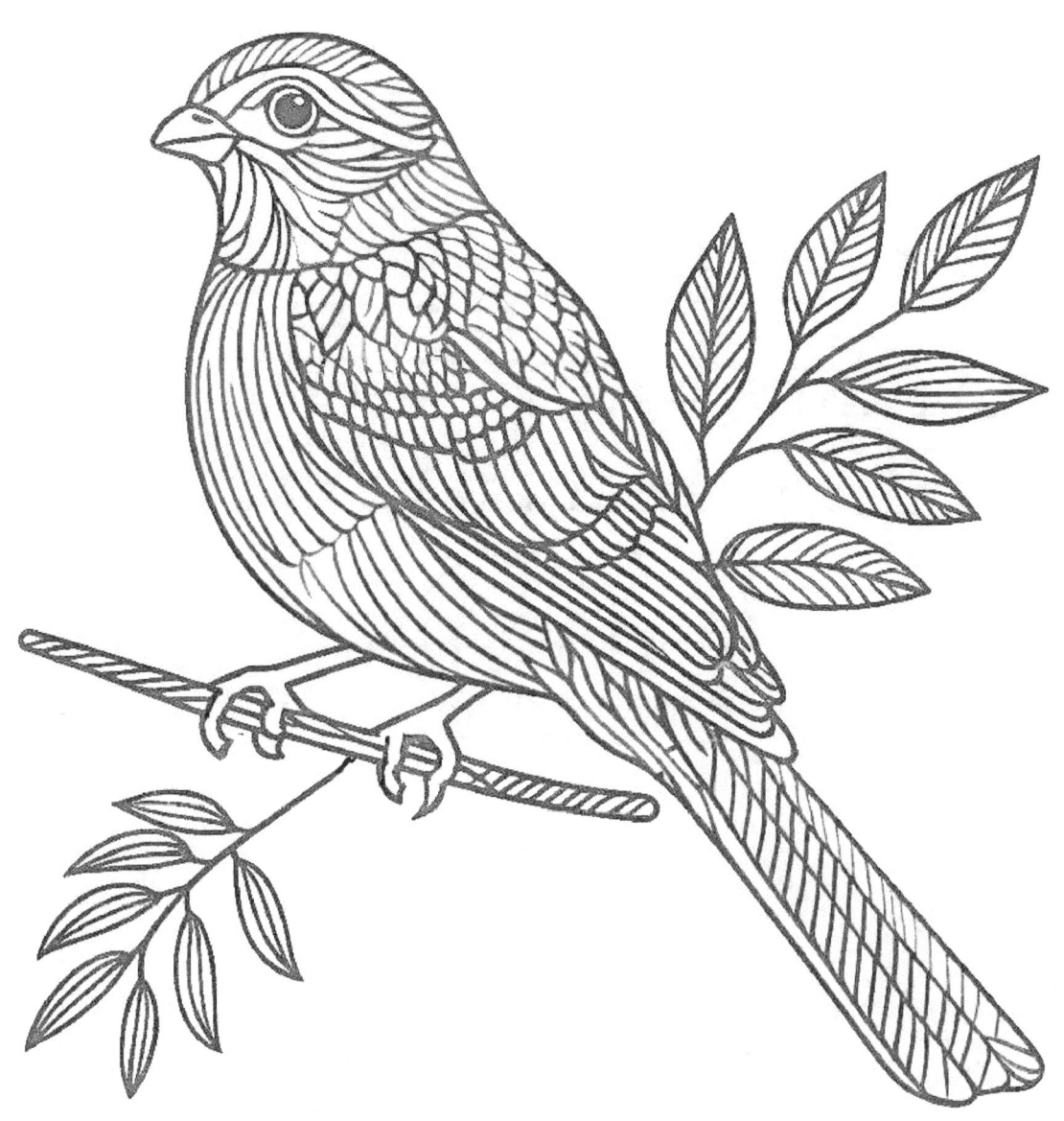

Flamingo

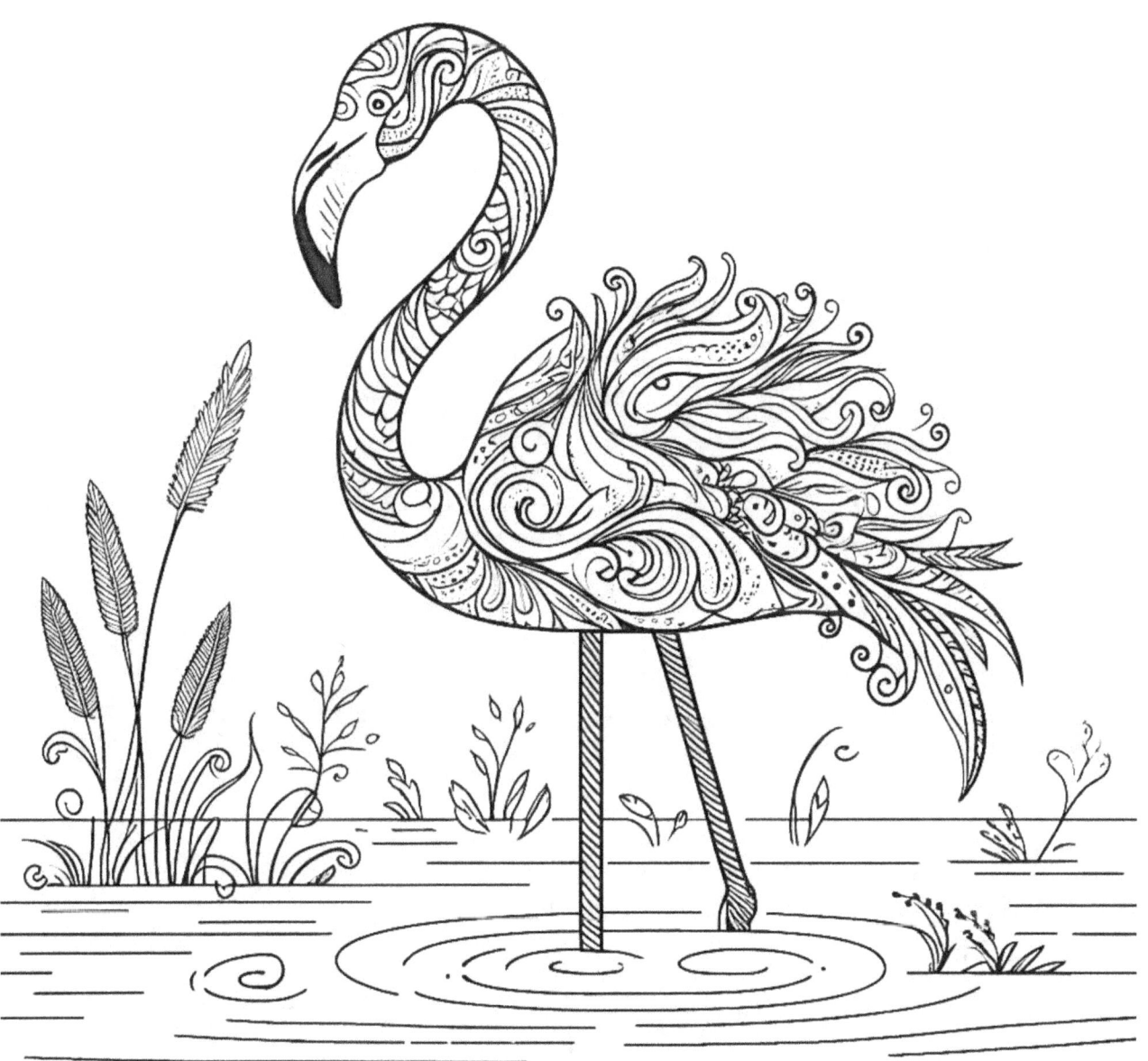

Sandpiper

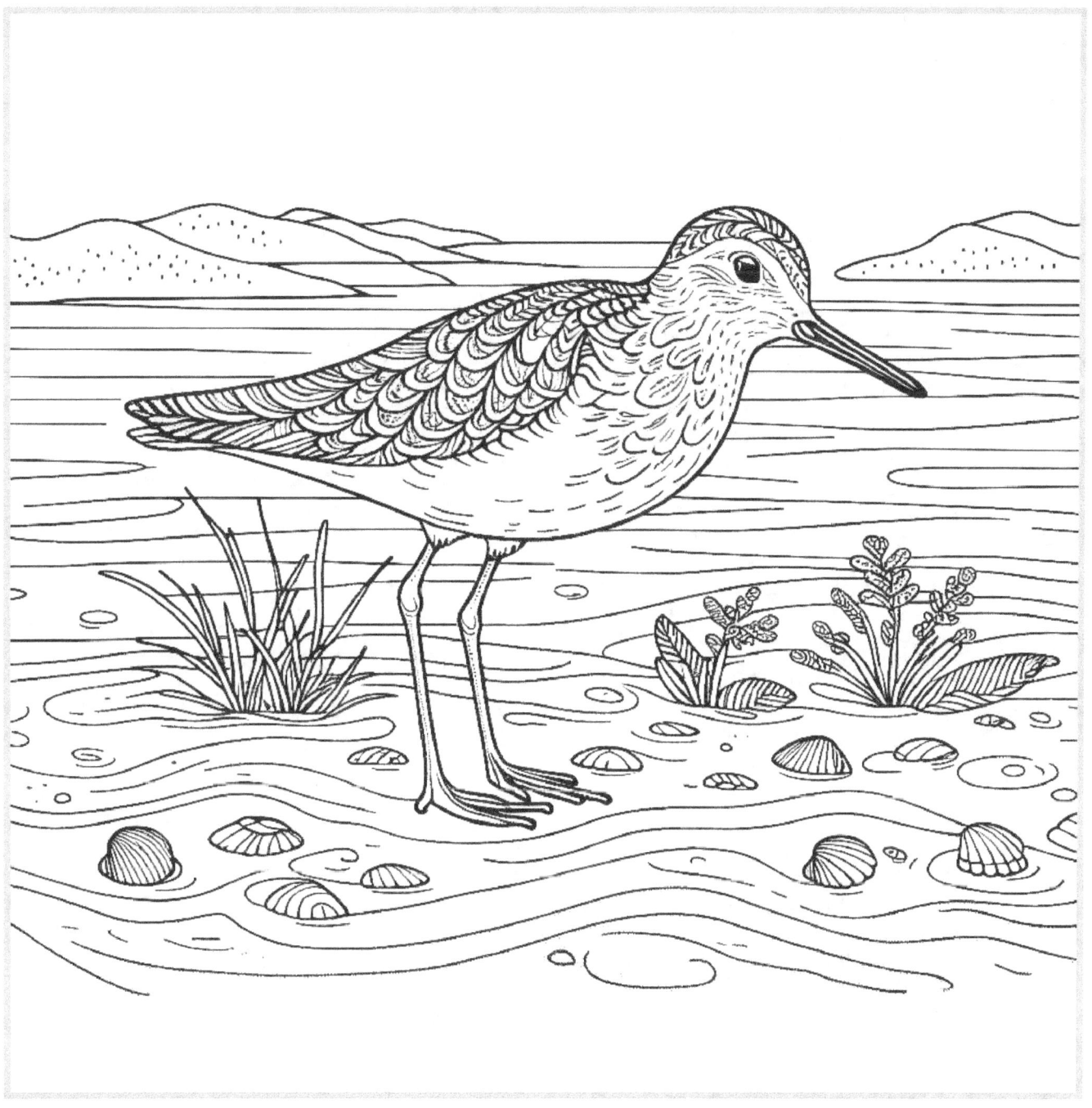

Northern Cardinal

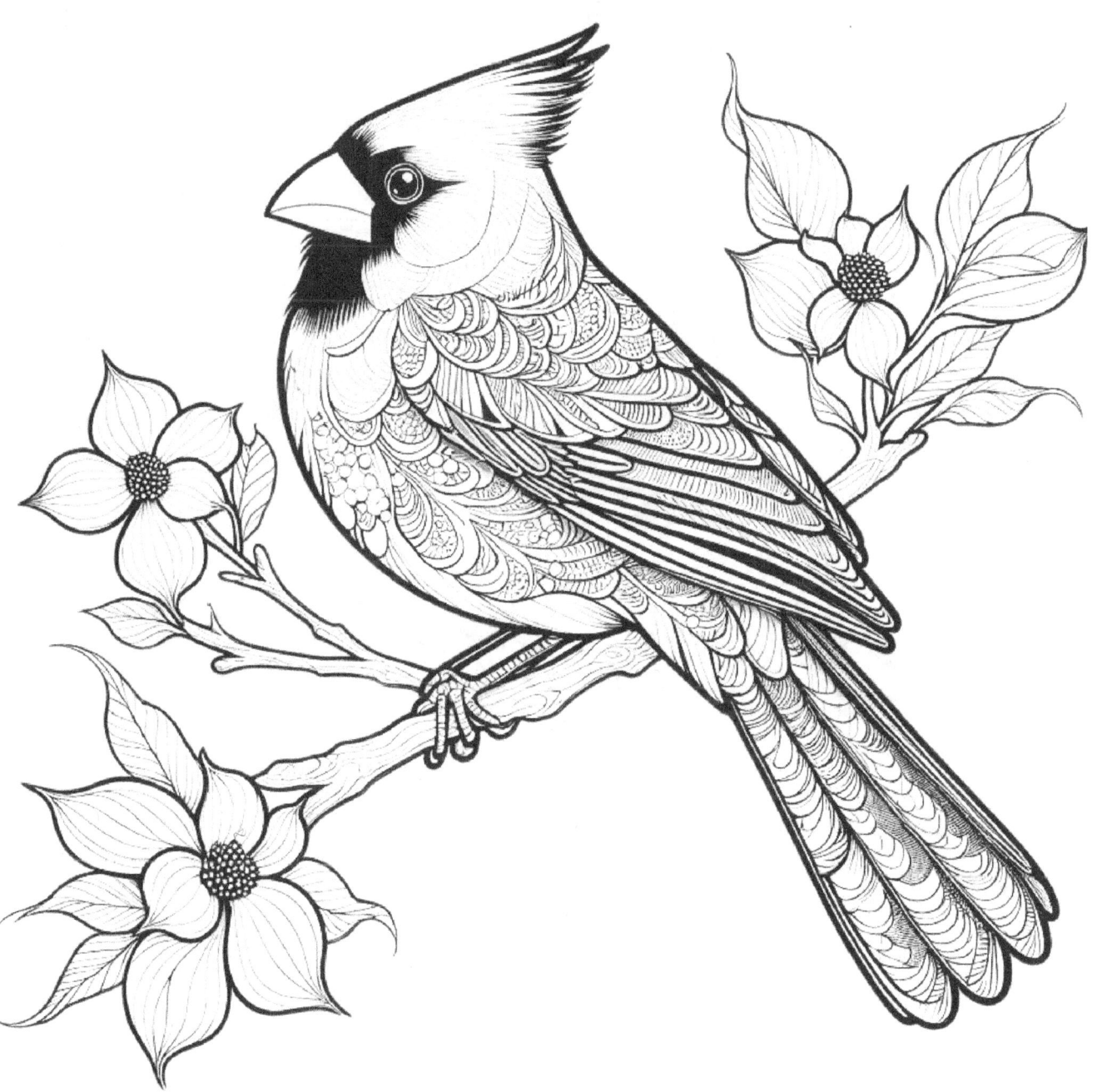

Snow Owl

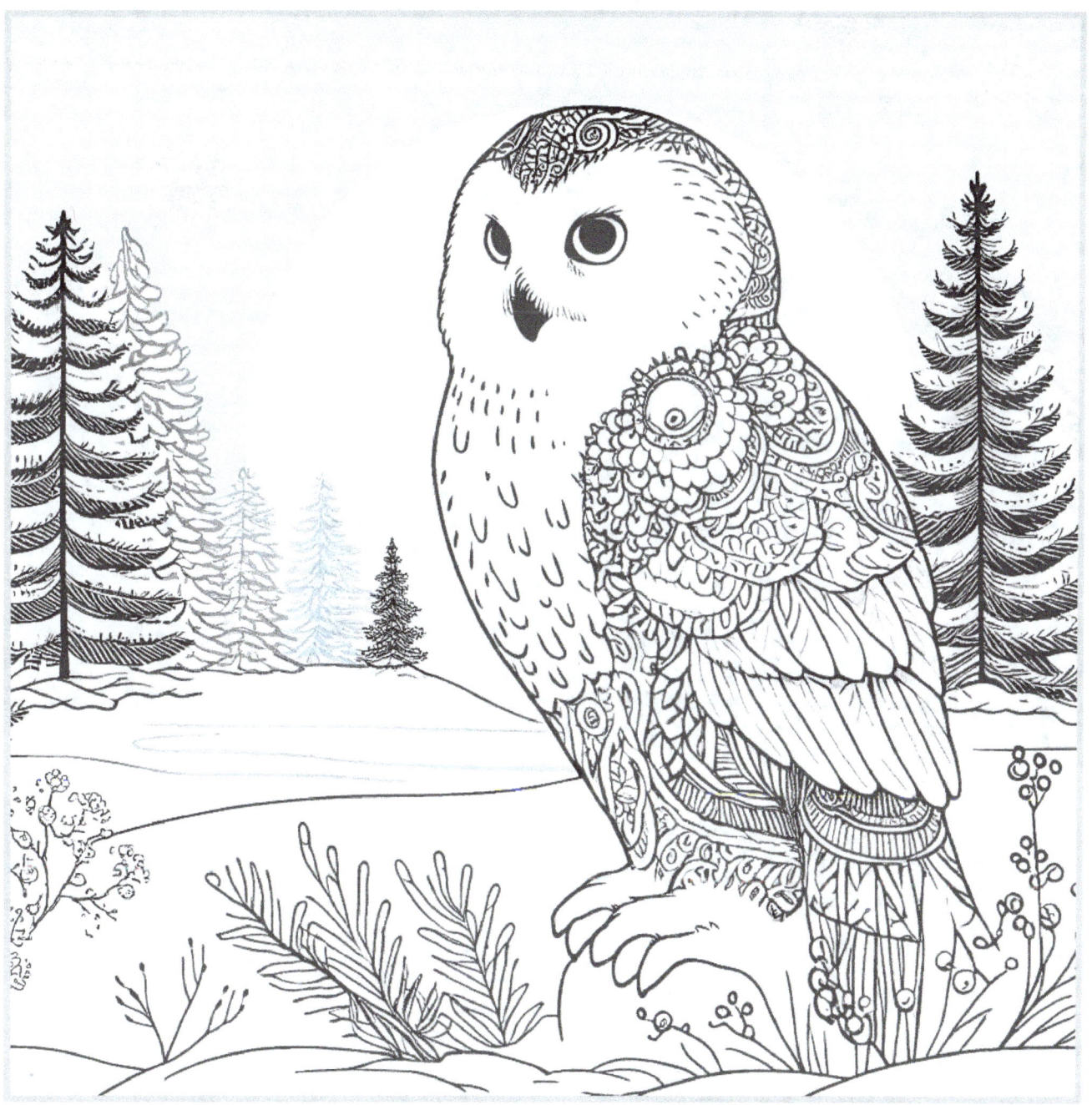

Peafowl

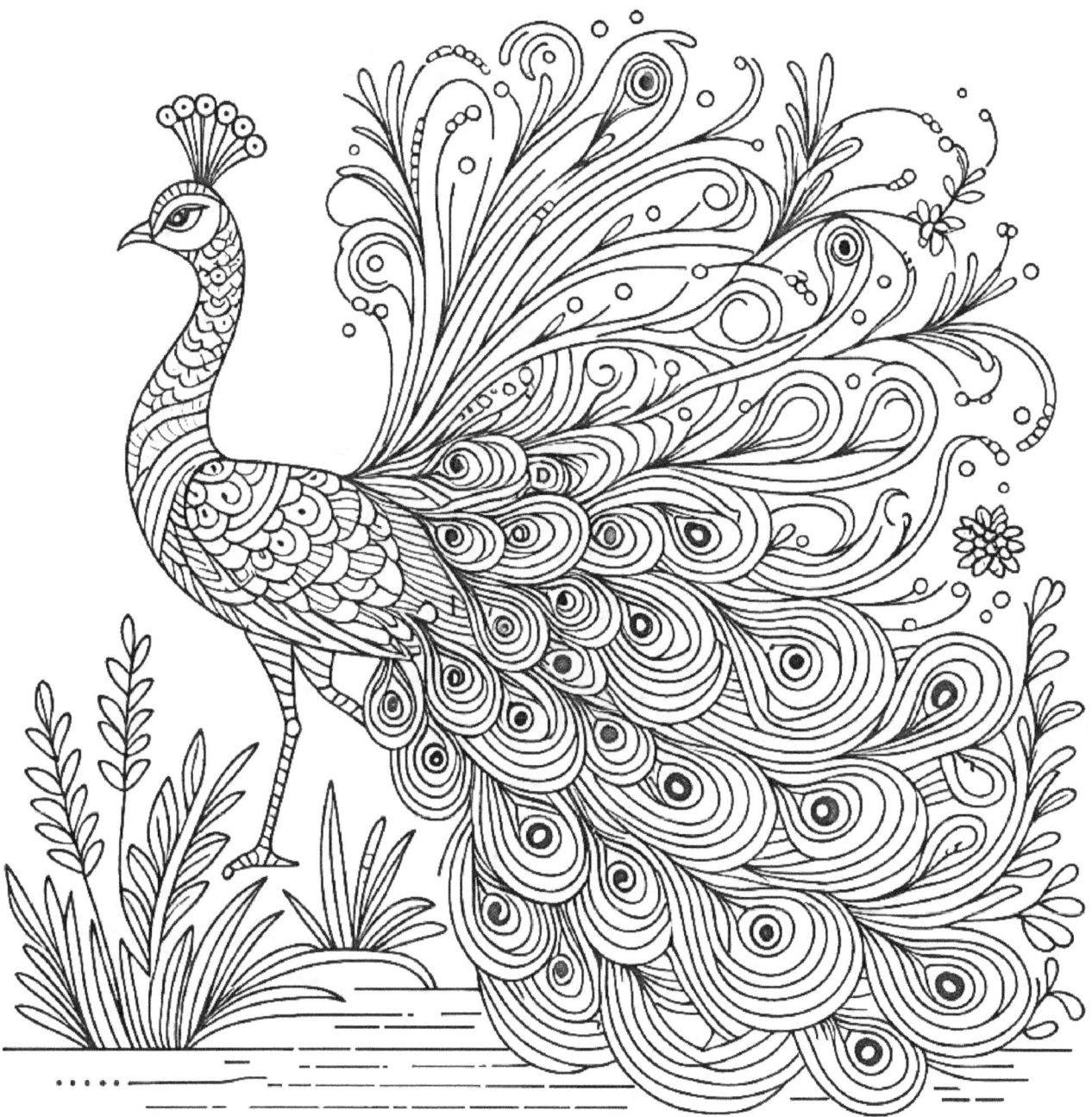

Hummingbird

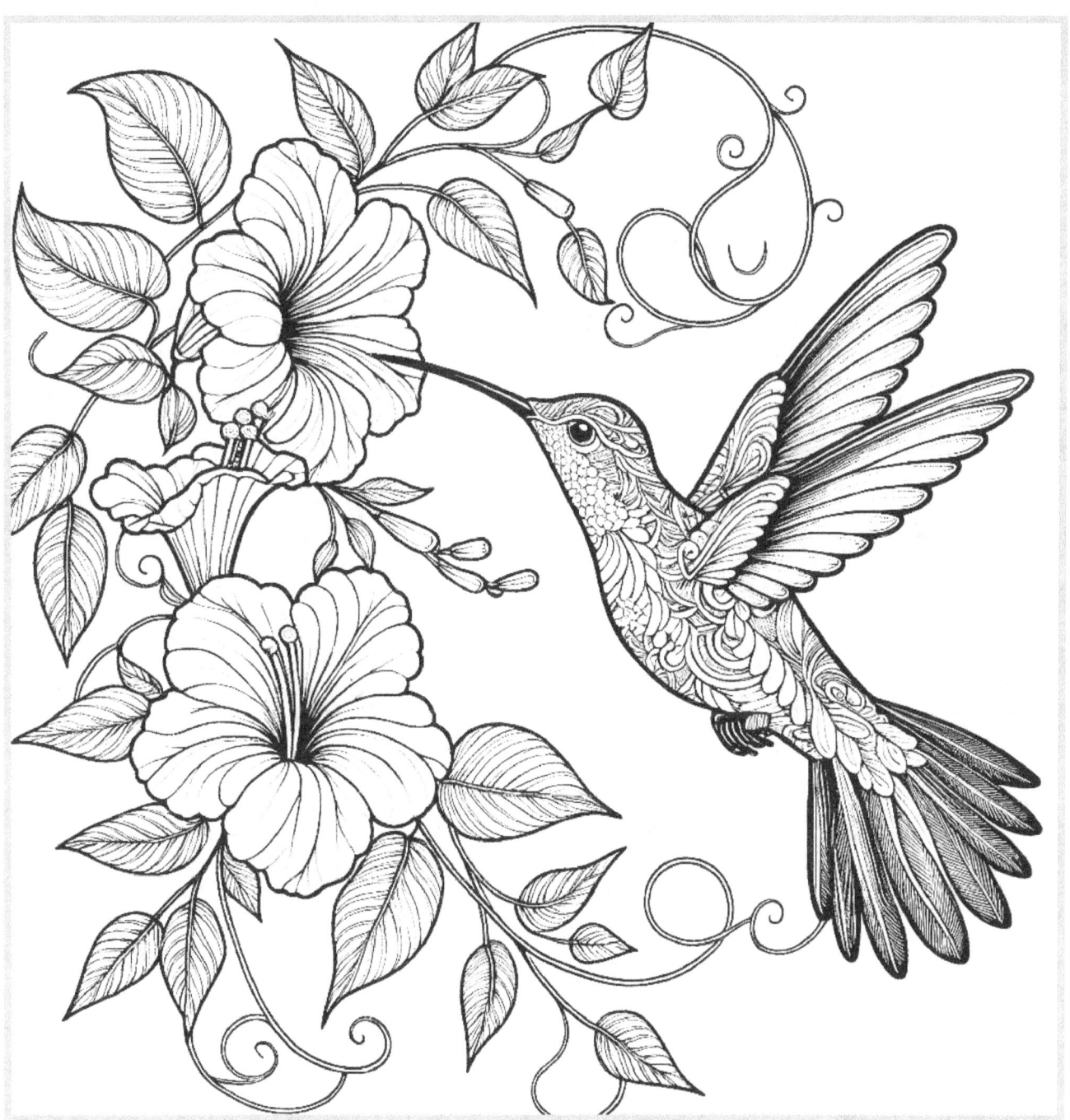

Mandarin Duck

Goldfinch

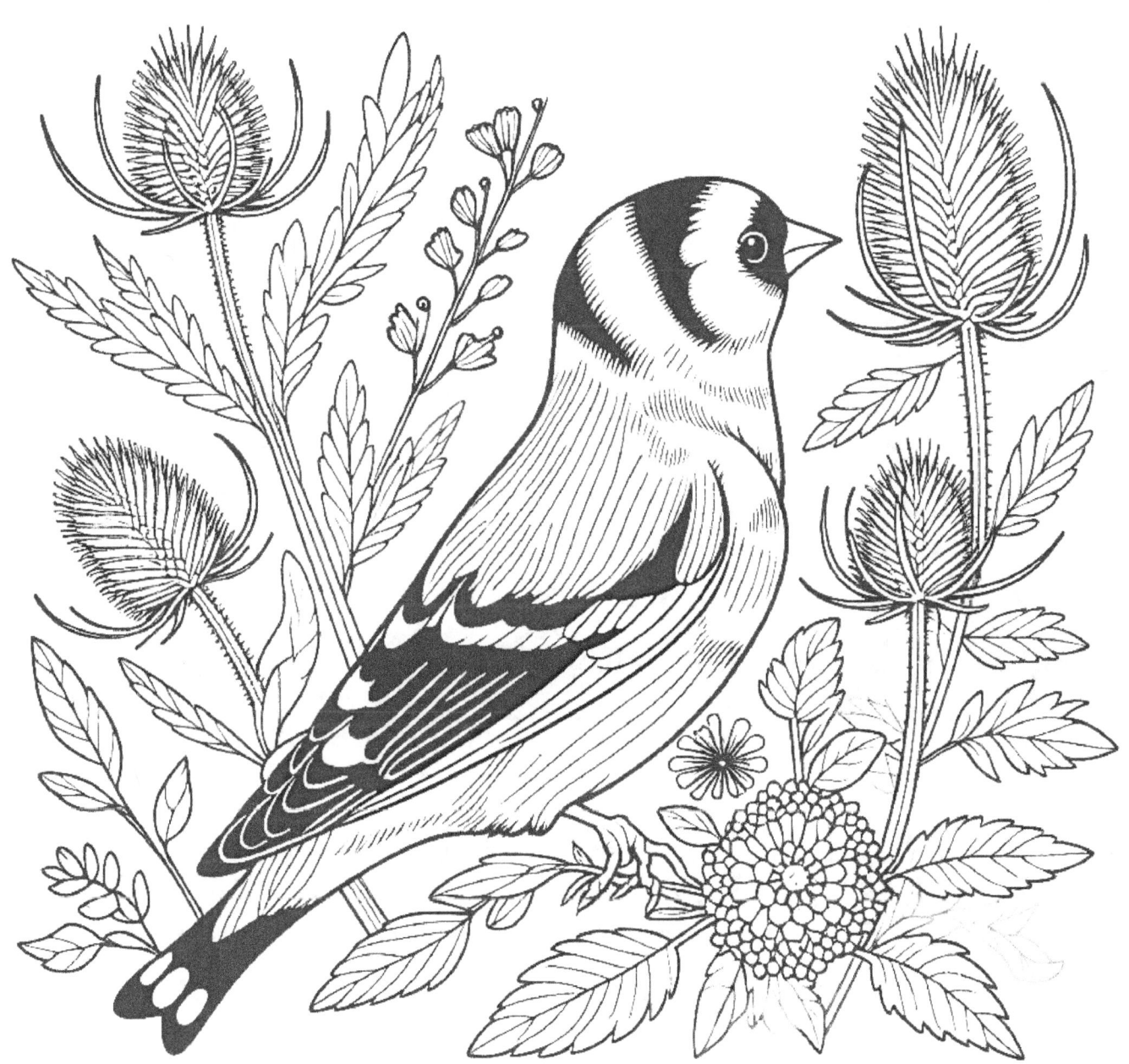

Toucan

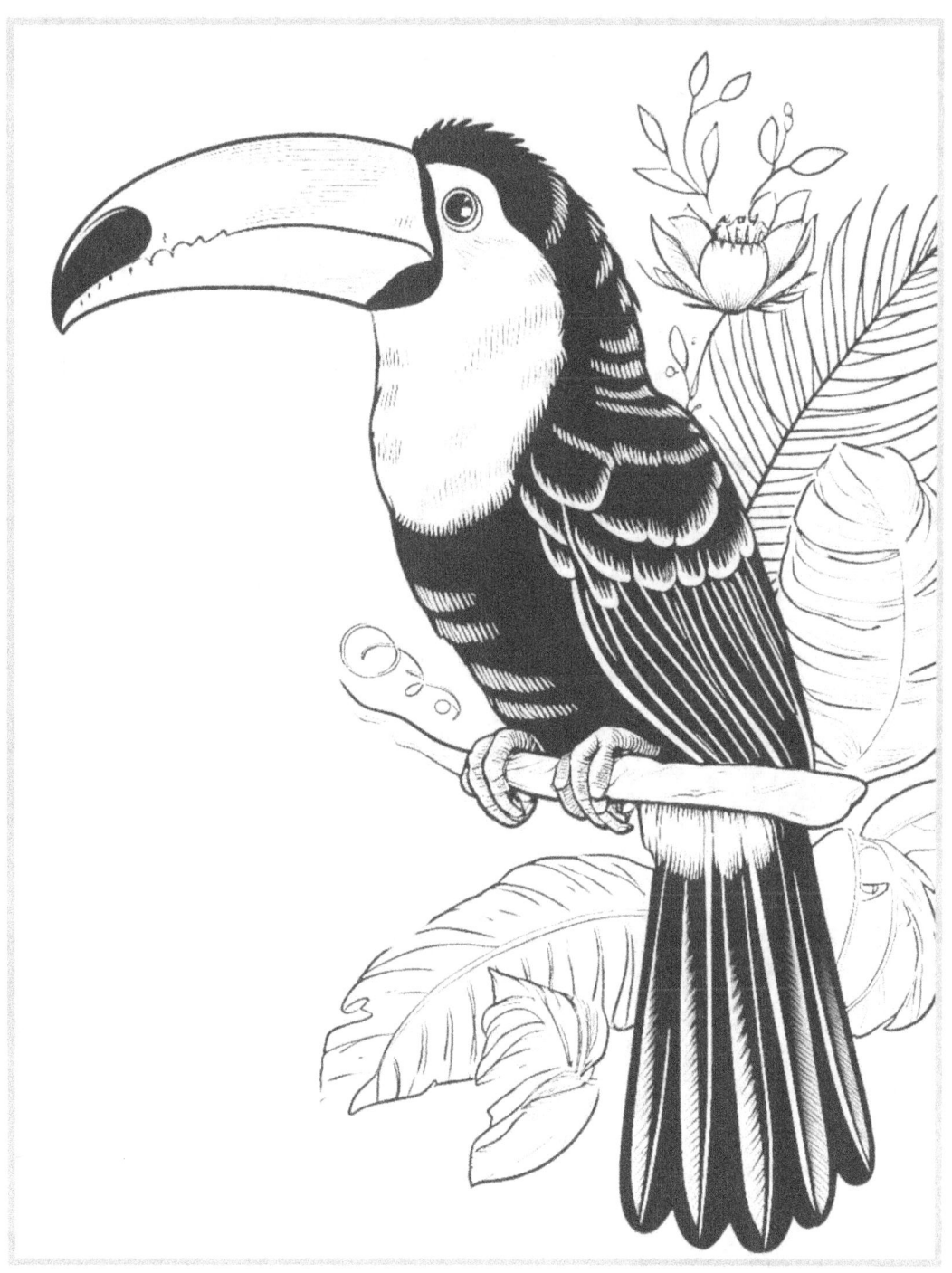

Indian Paradise Flycatcher

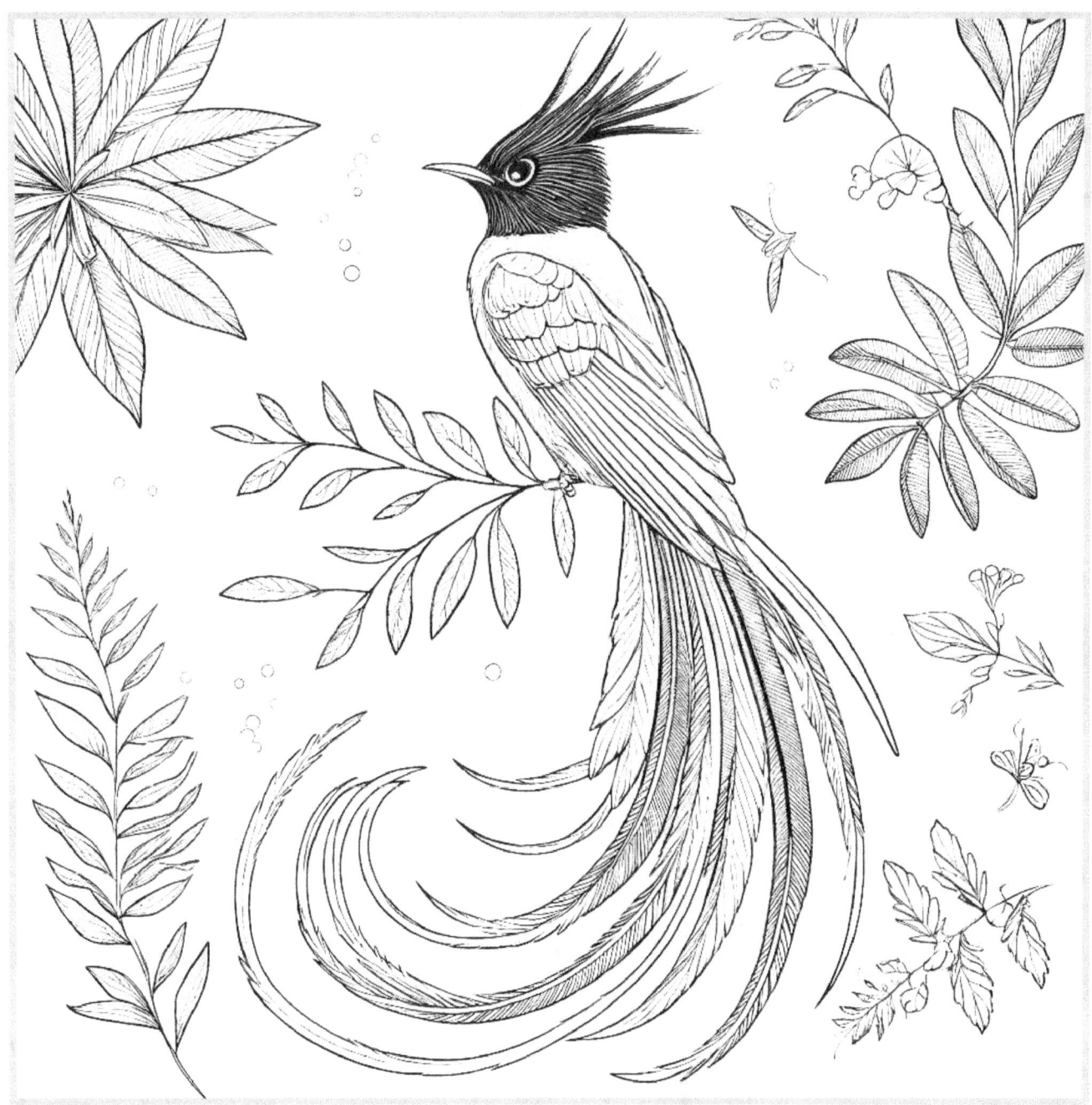

Greater Roadrunner

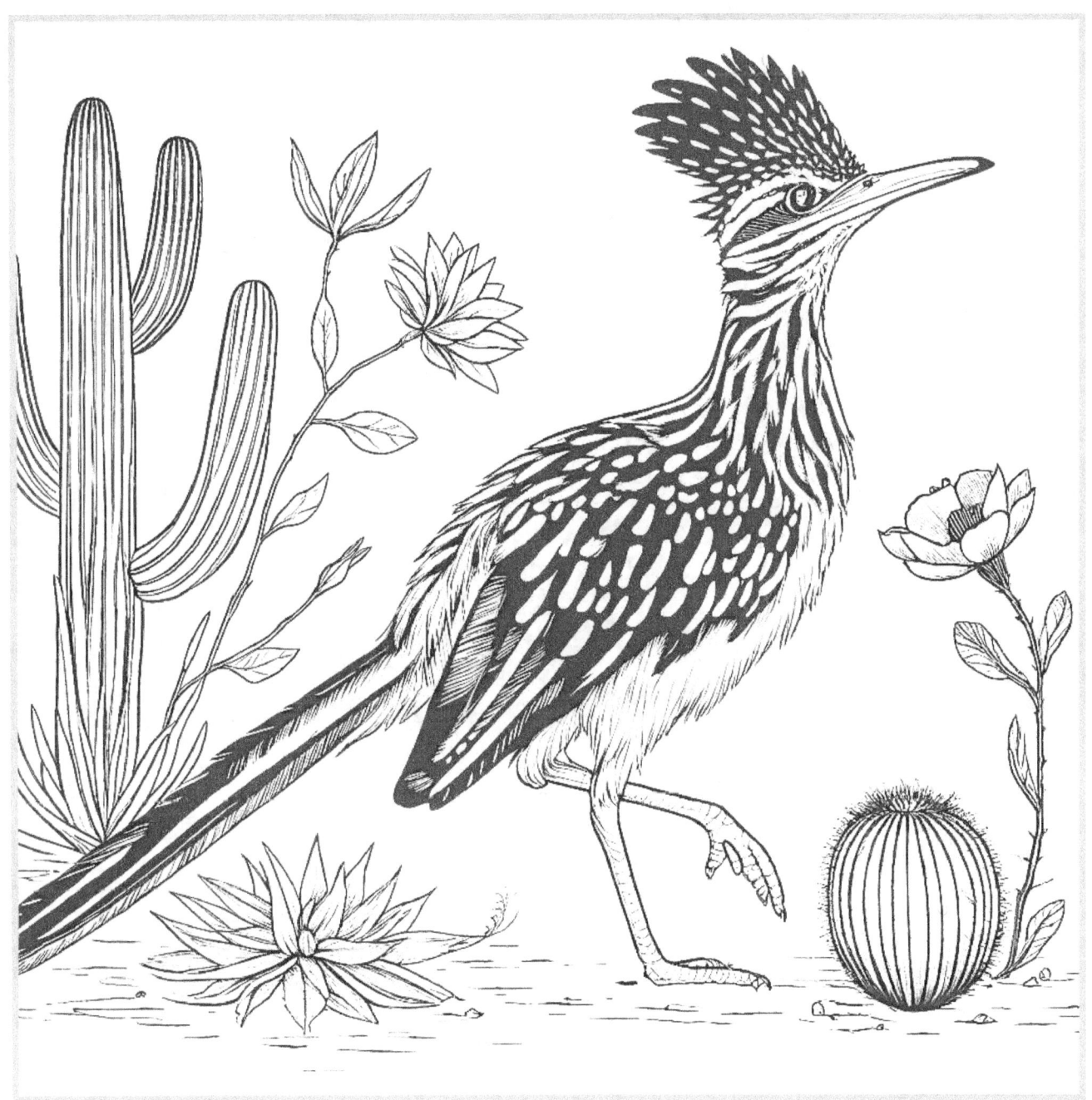

Kea

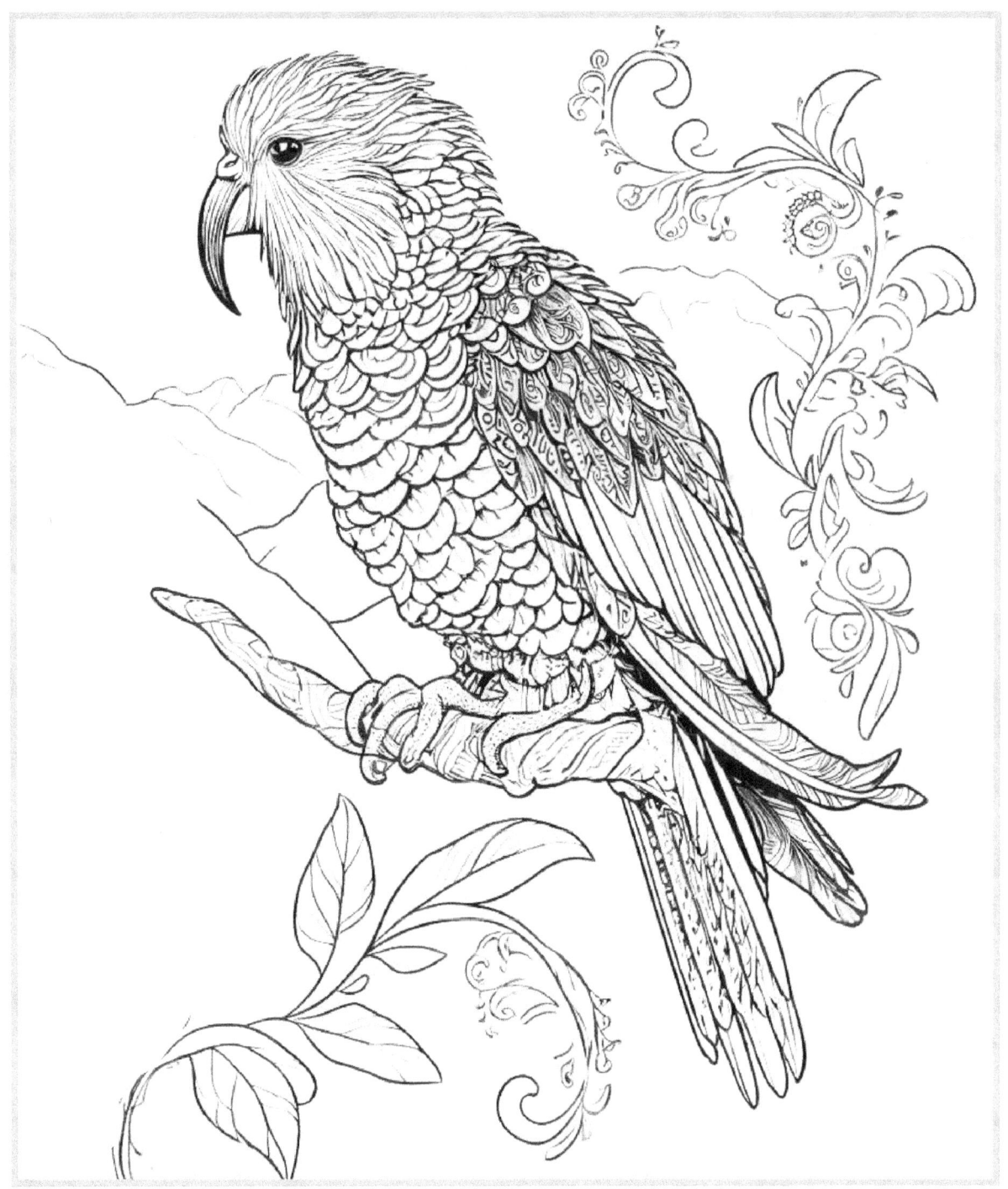

Spoonbill

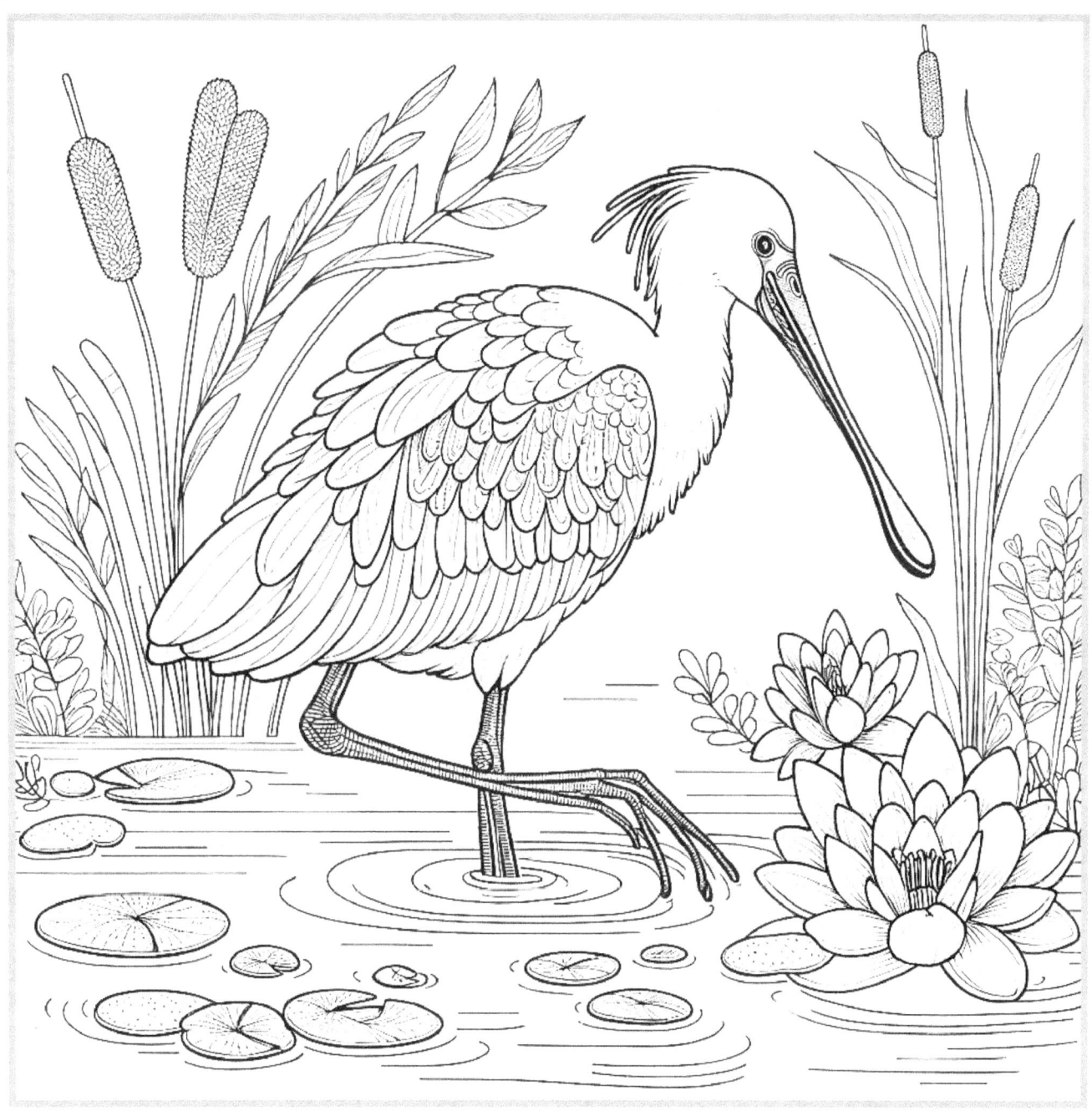

Turquoise-browed Motmot

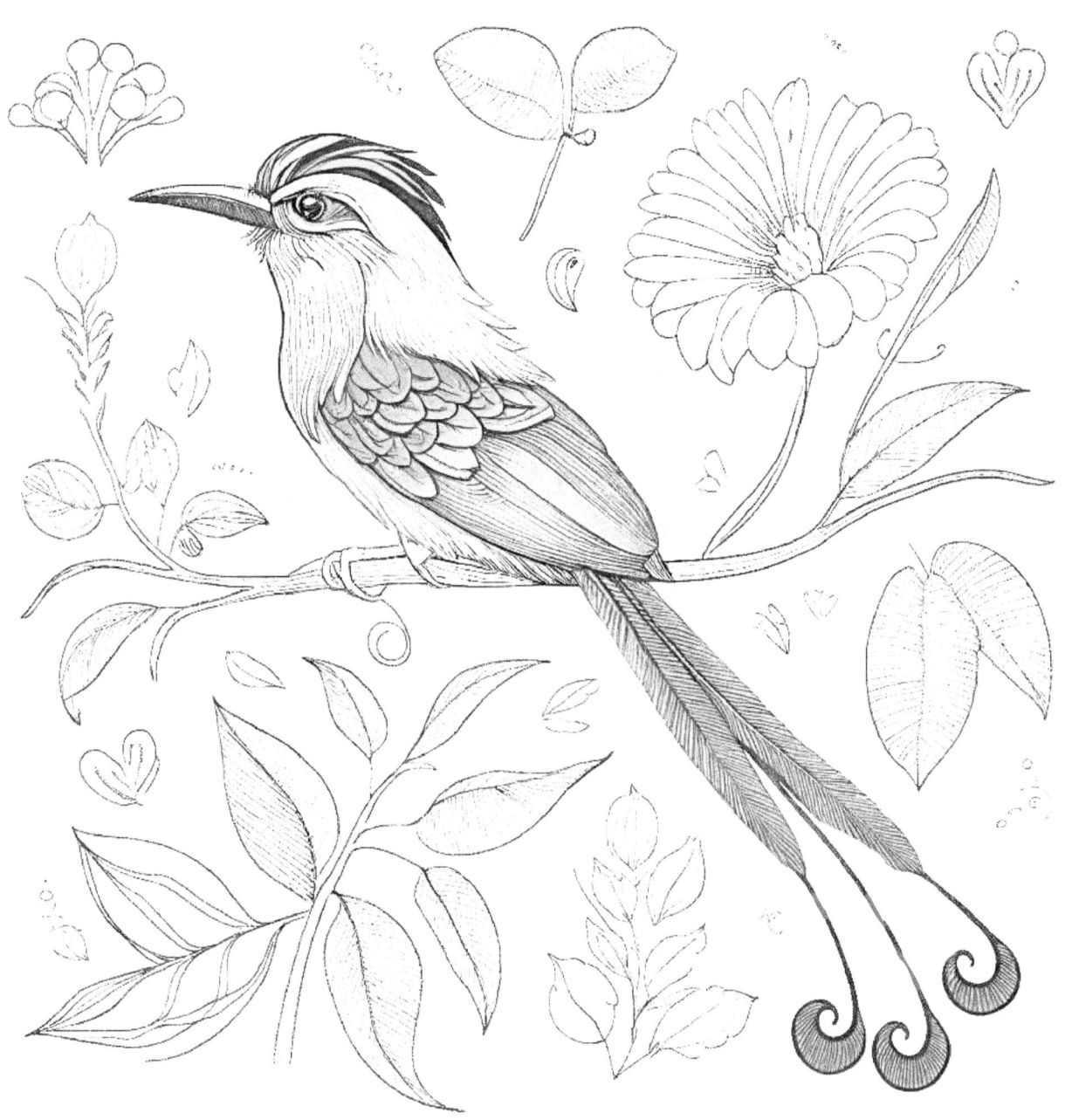

Waved Albatross

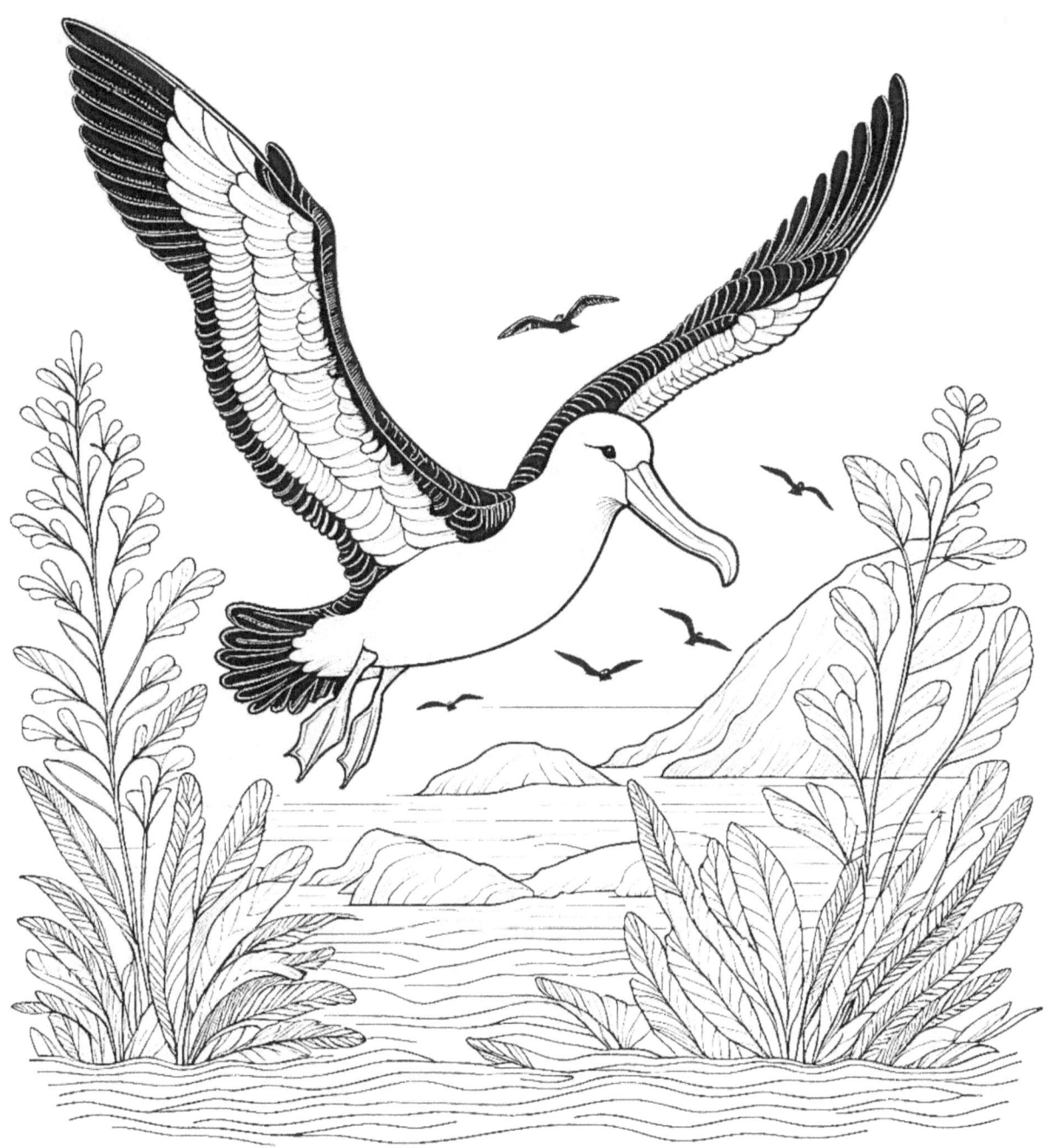

Amazonian Royal Flycatcher

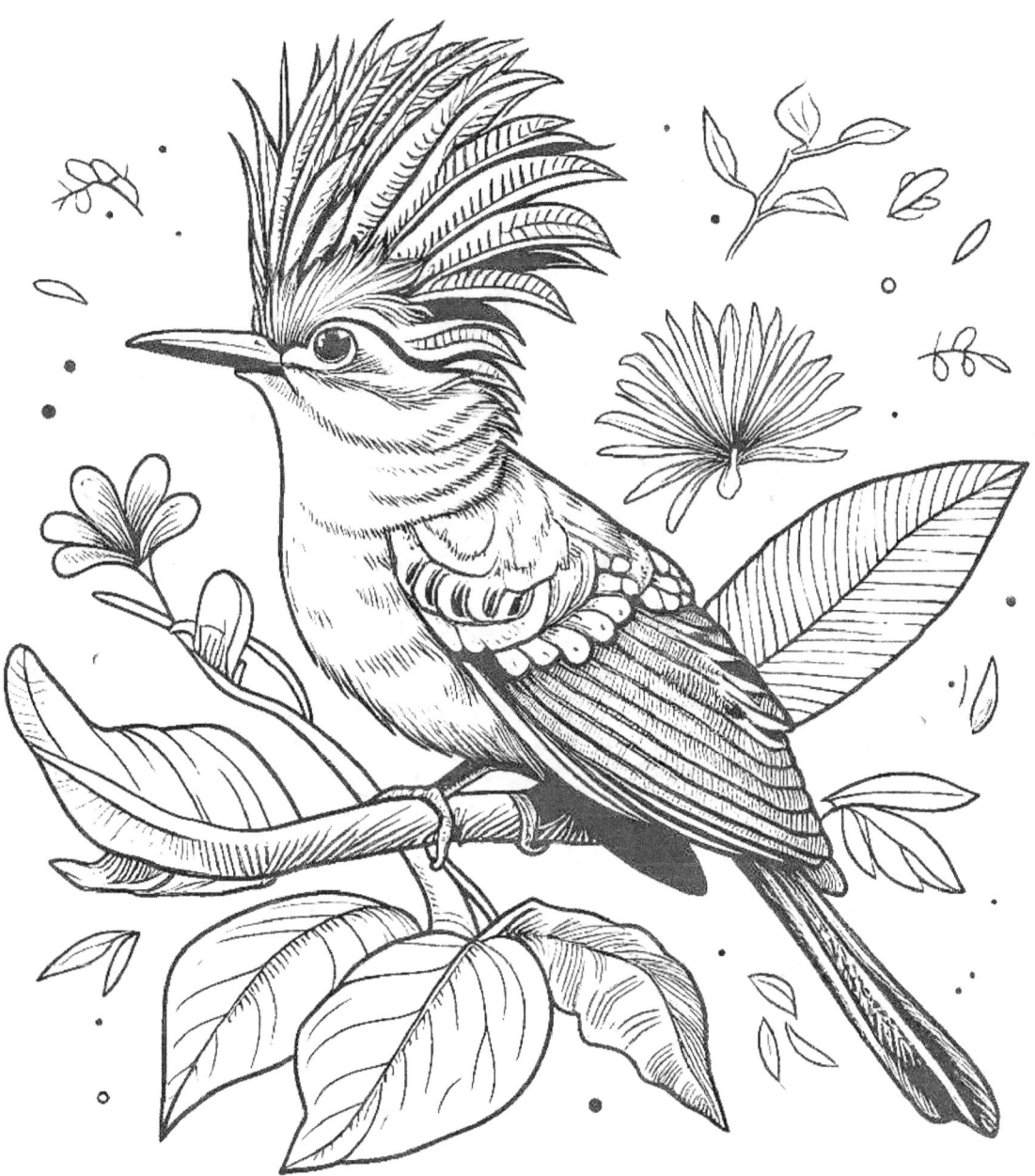

Wild Turkey

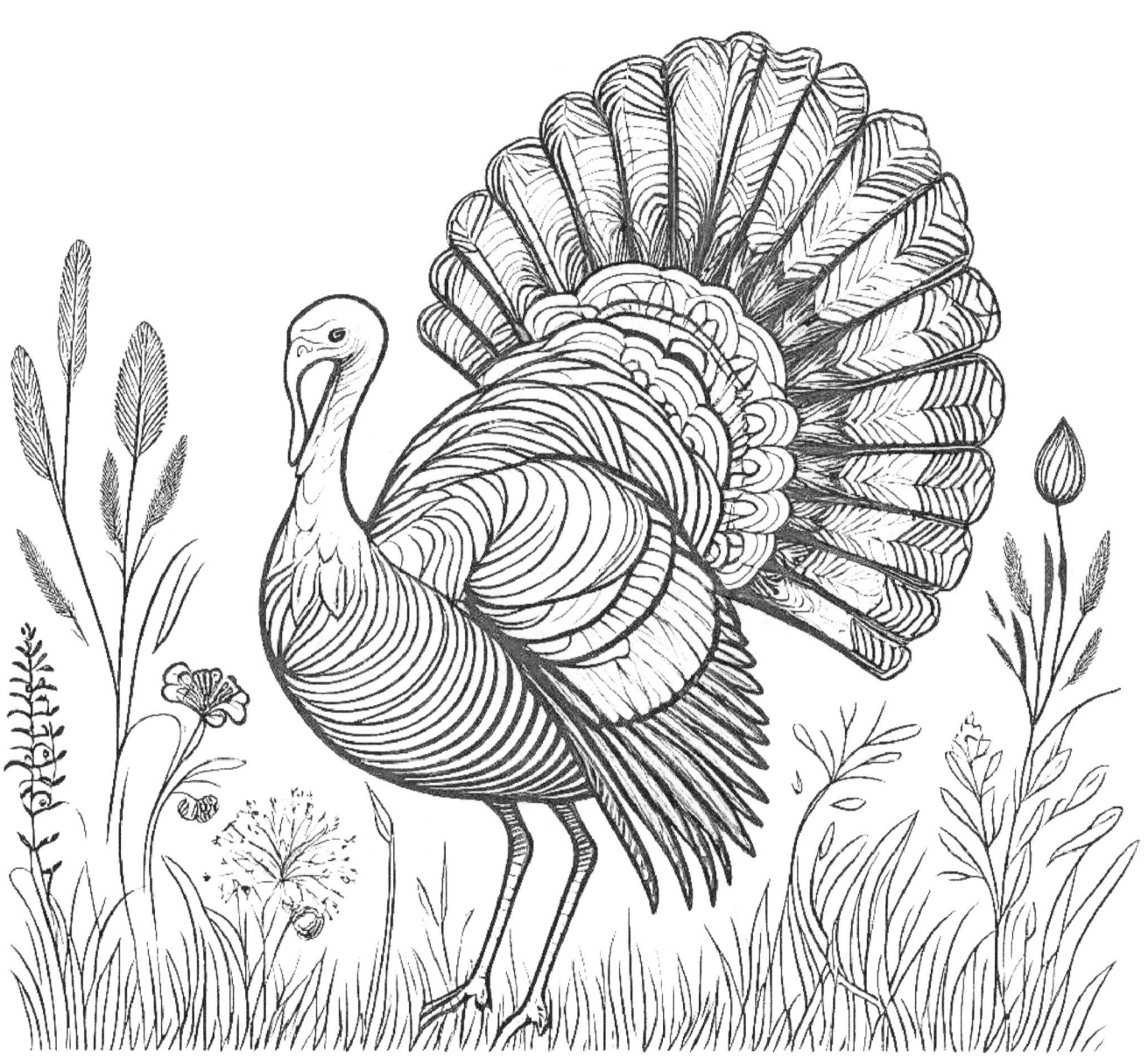

Scissor-Tailed Flycatcher

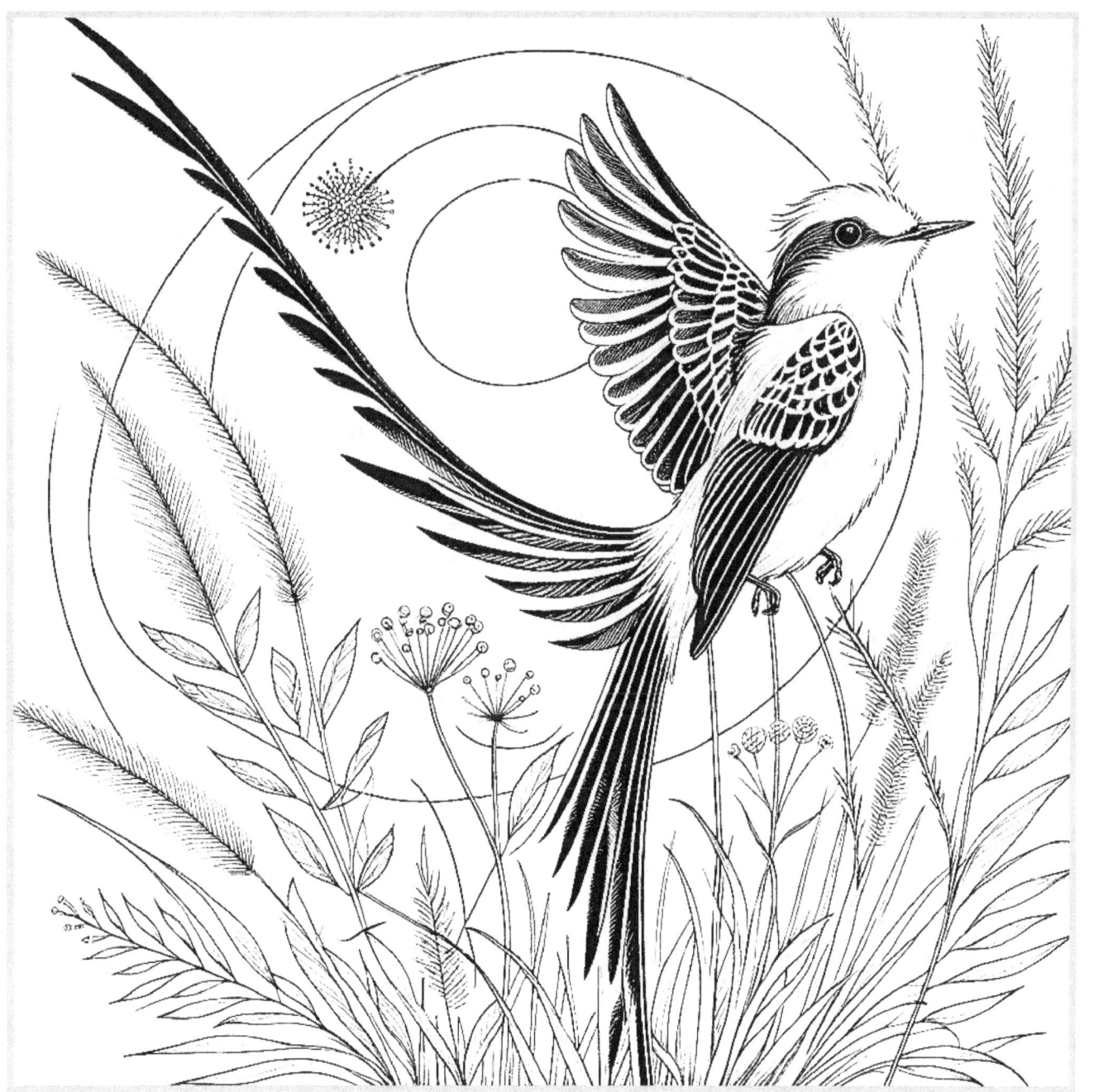

New Caledonian Owlet-Nightjar

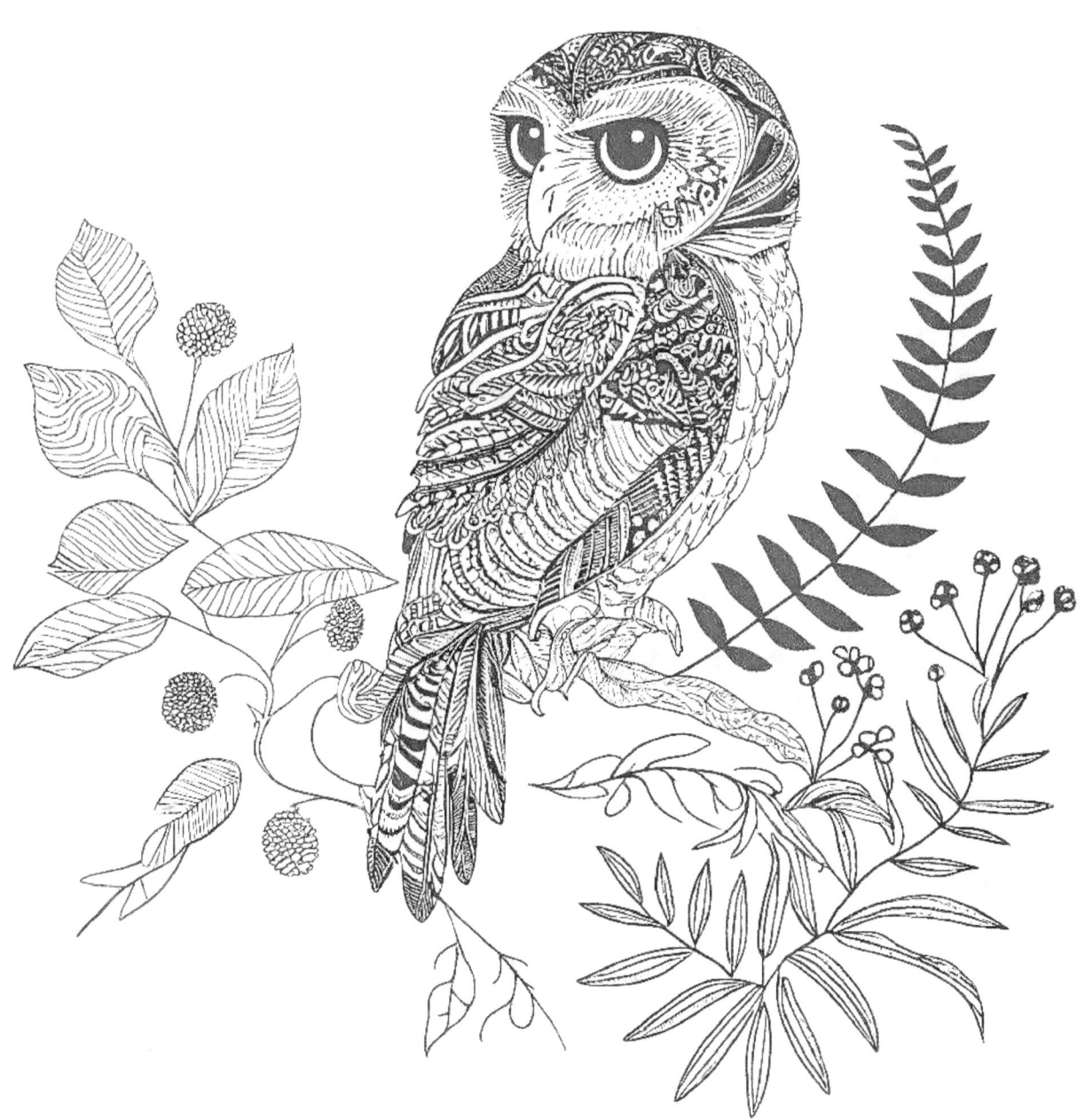

Golden Pheasant

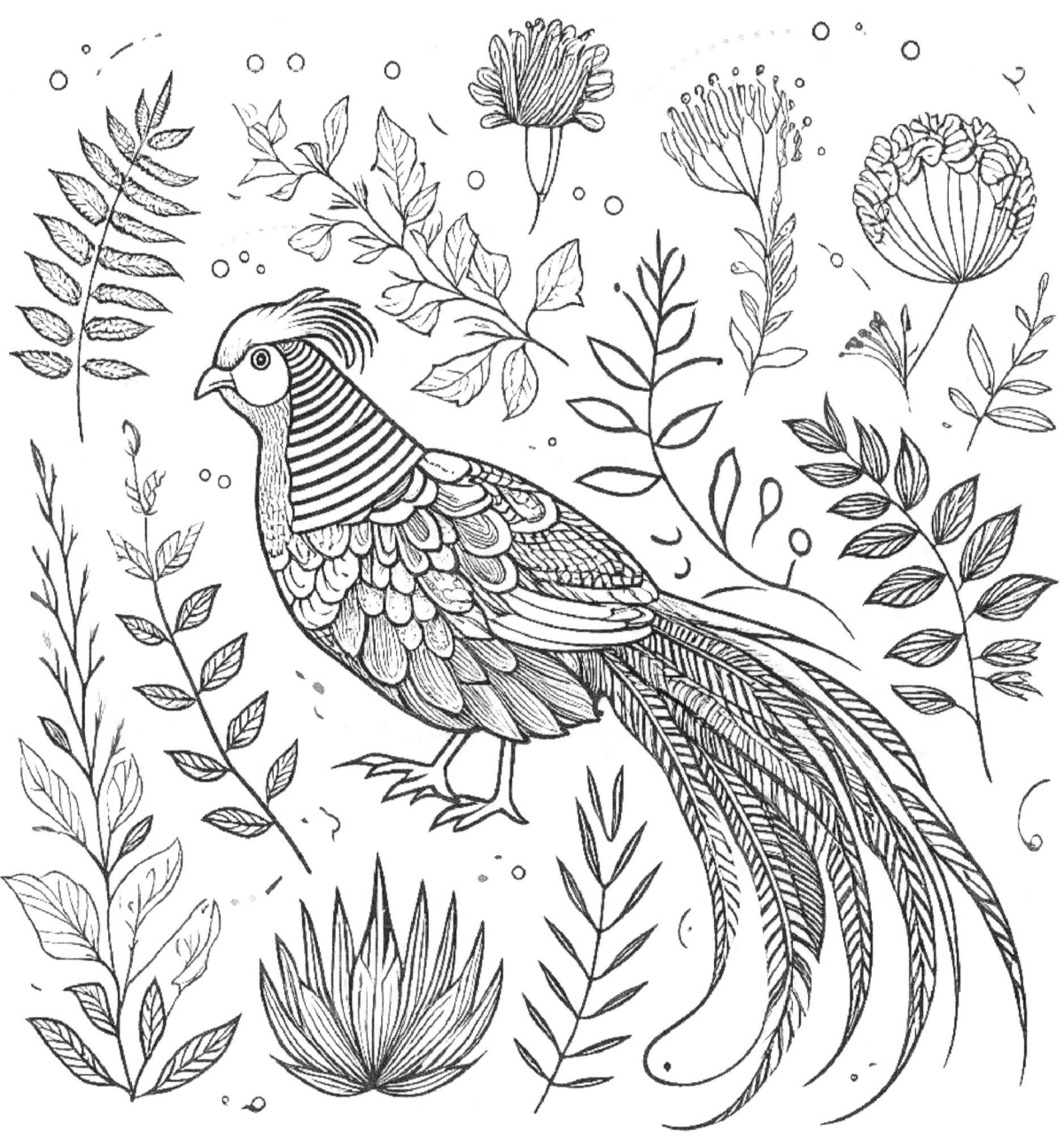

Eurasian Hoopoe

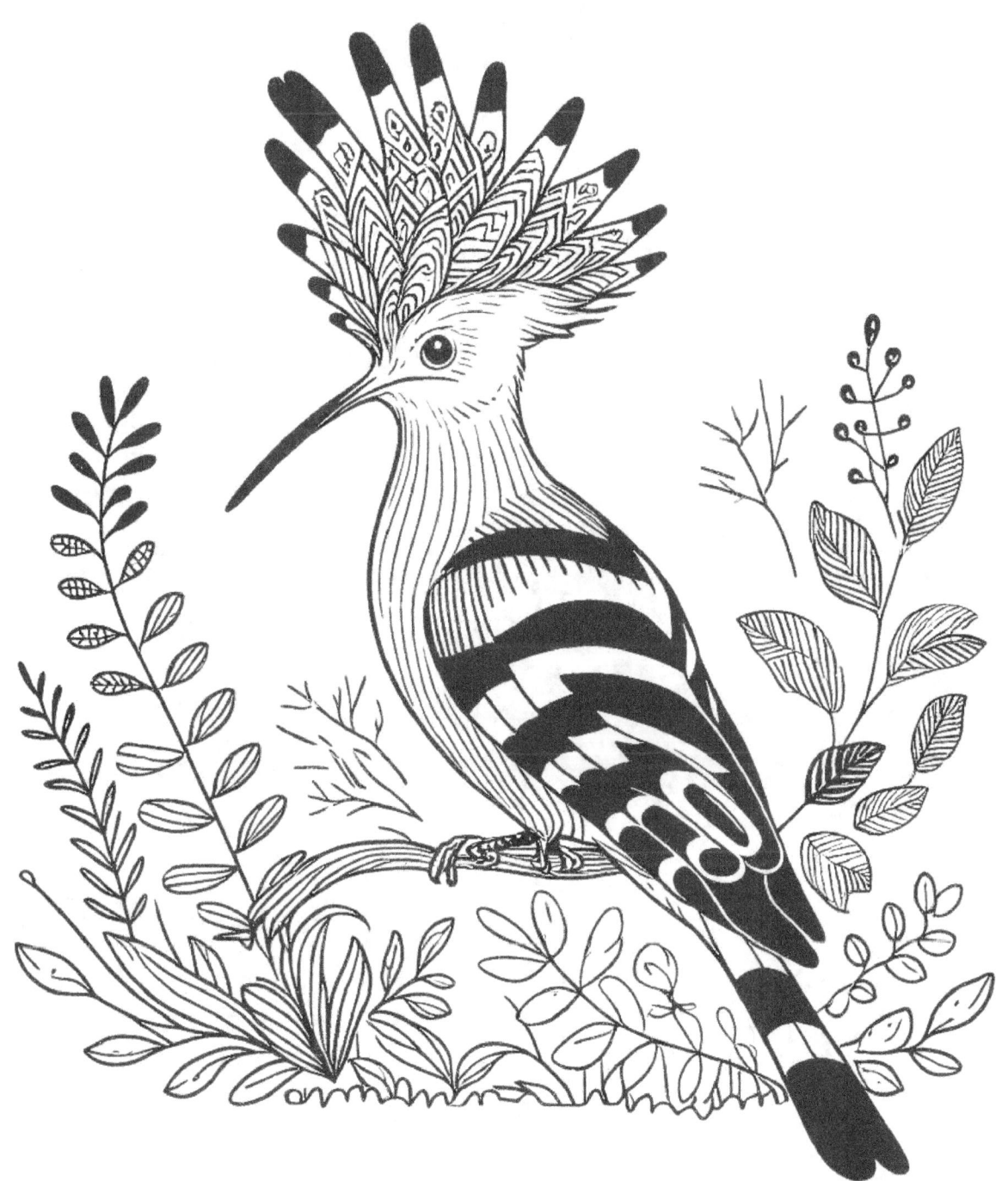

Imperial Amazon

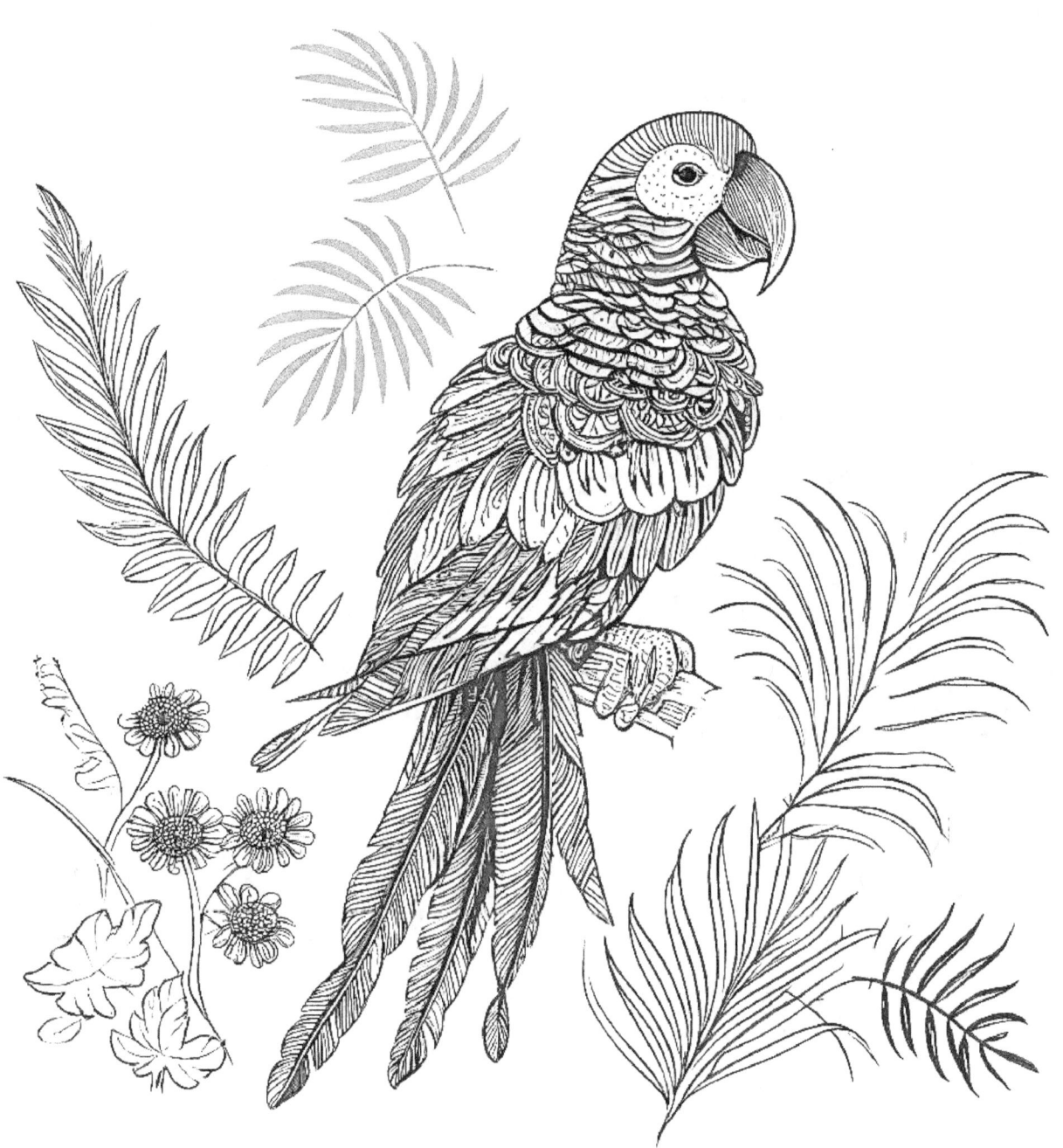

Grey Crowned Crane

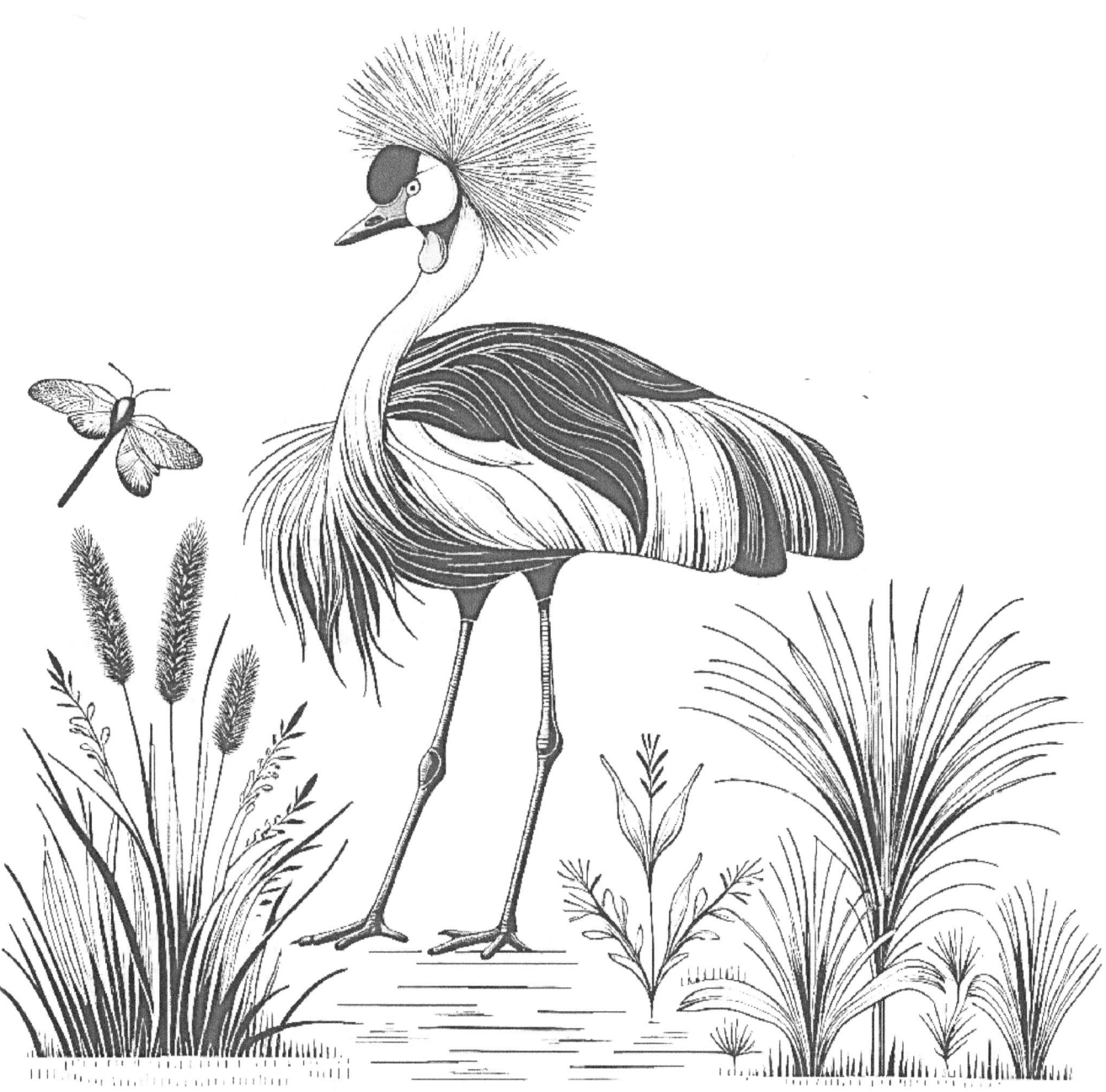

Superb Lyrebird

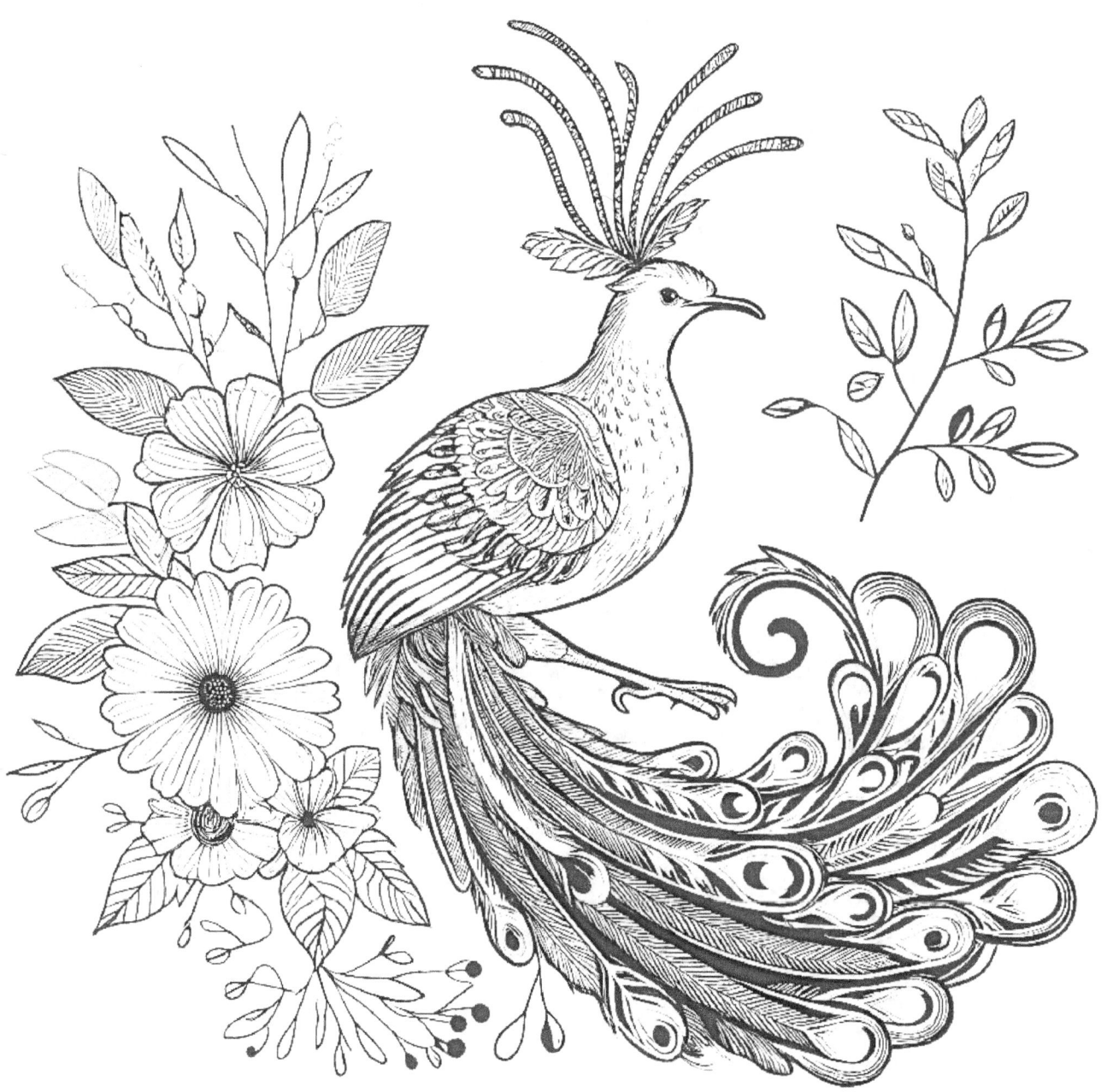

Lady Amherst's Pheasant

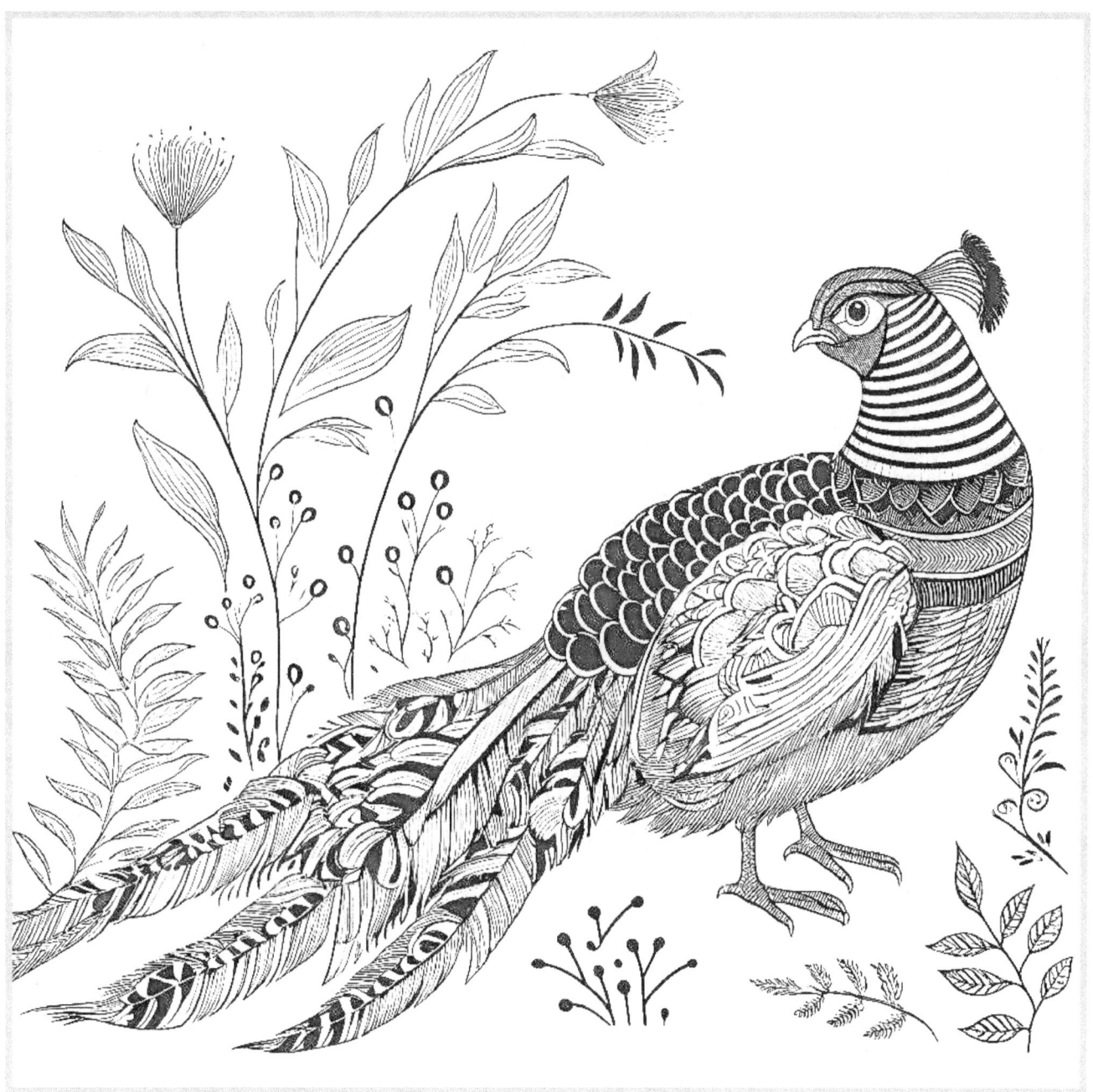

King of Saxony Bird-of-Paradise

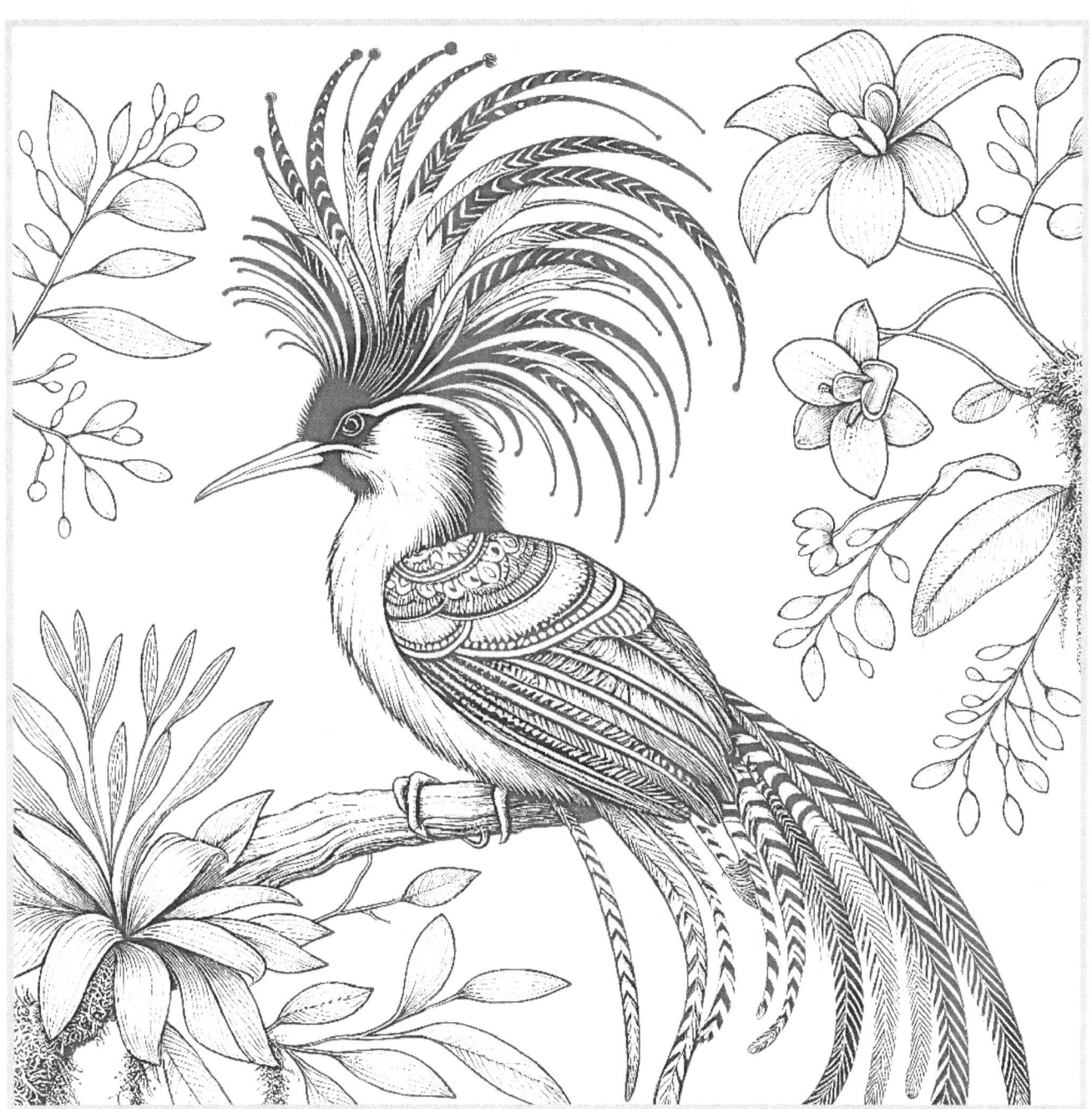

Giant Ibis

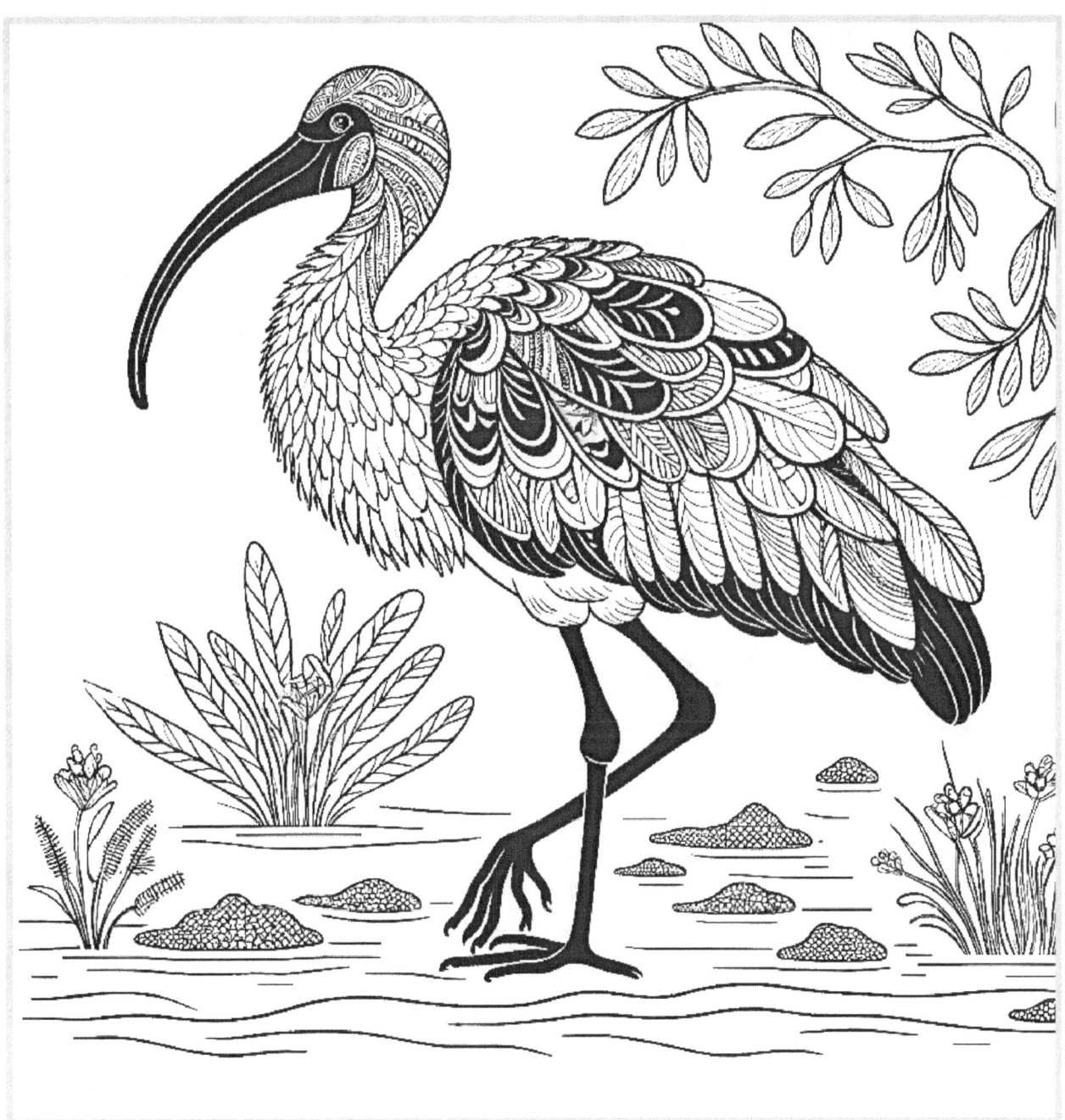

Resplendent Quetzal

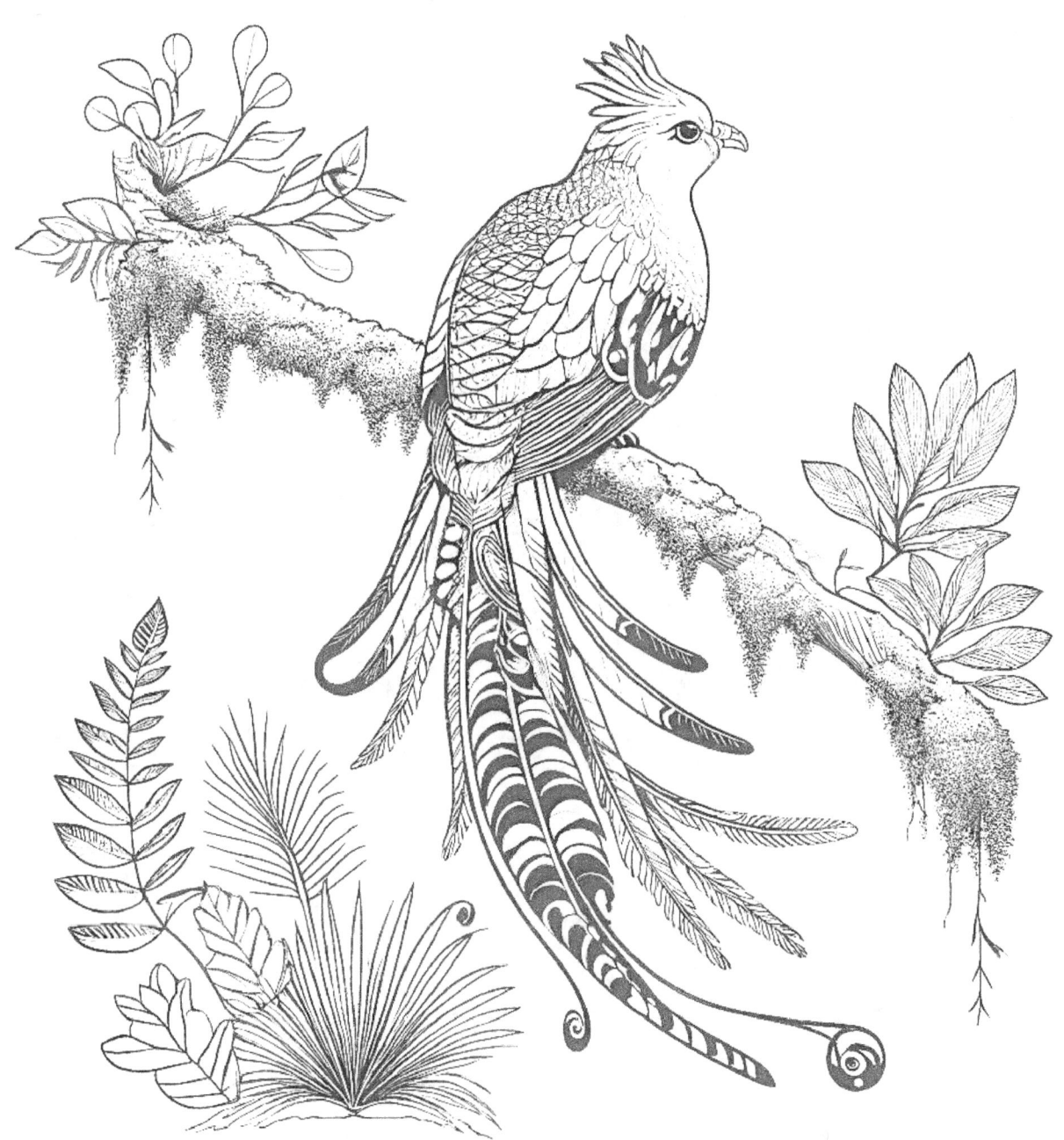

Great Blue Heron

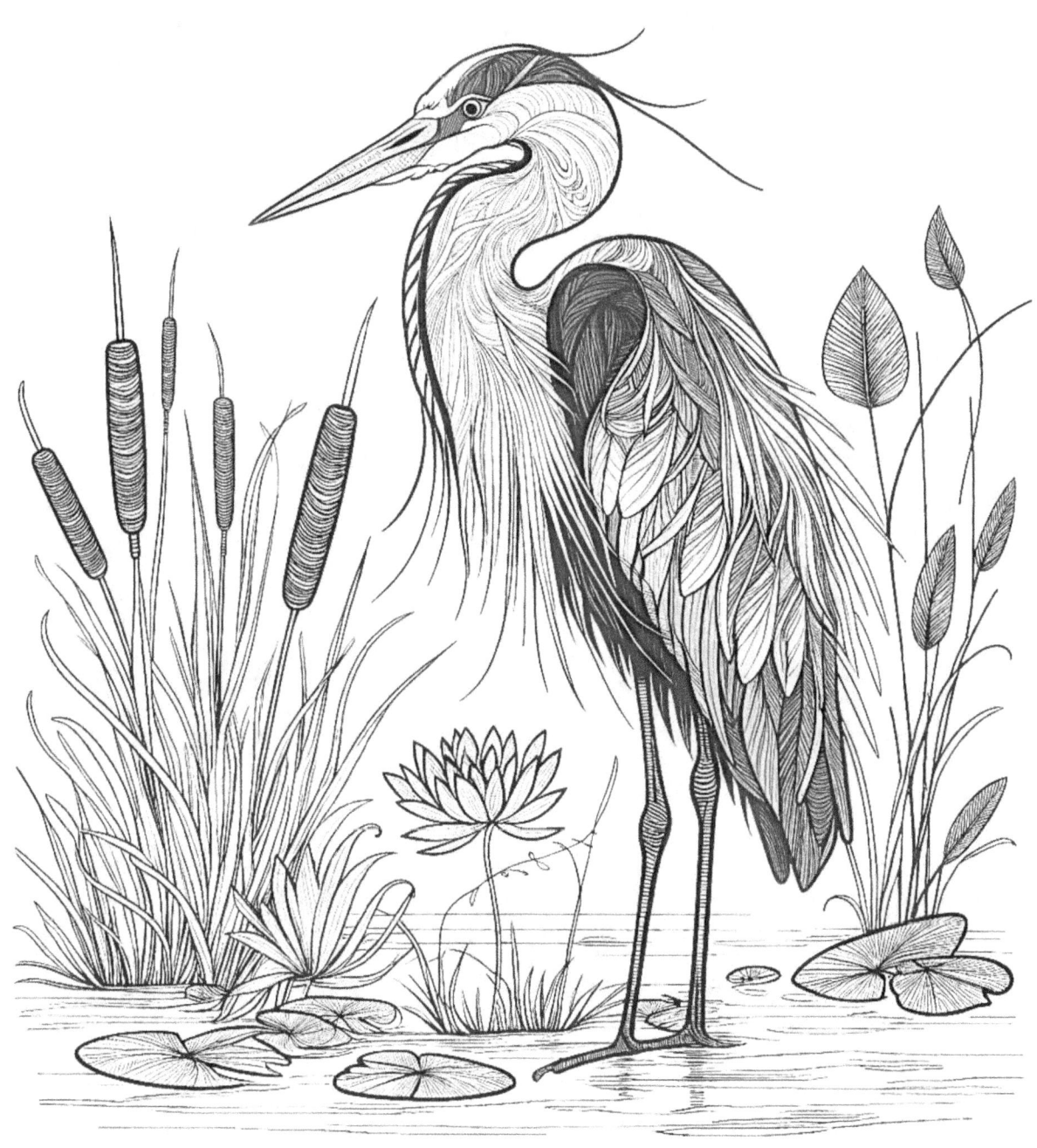

Long-Tailed Widowbird

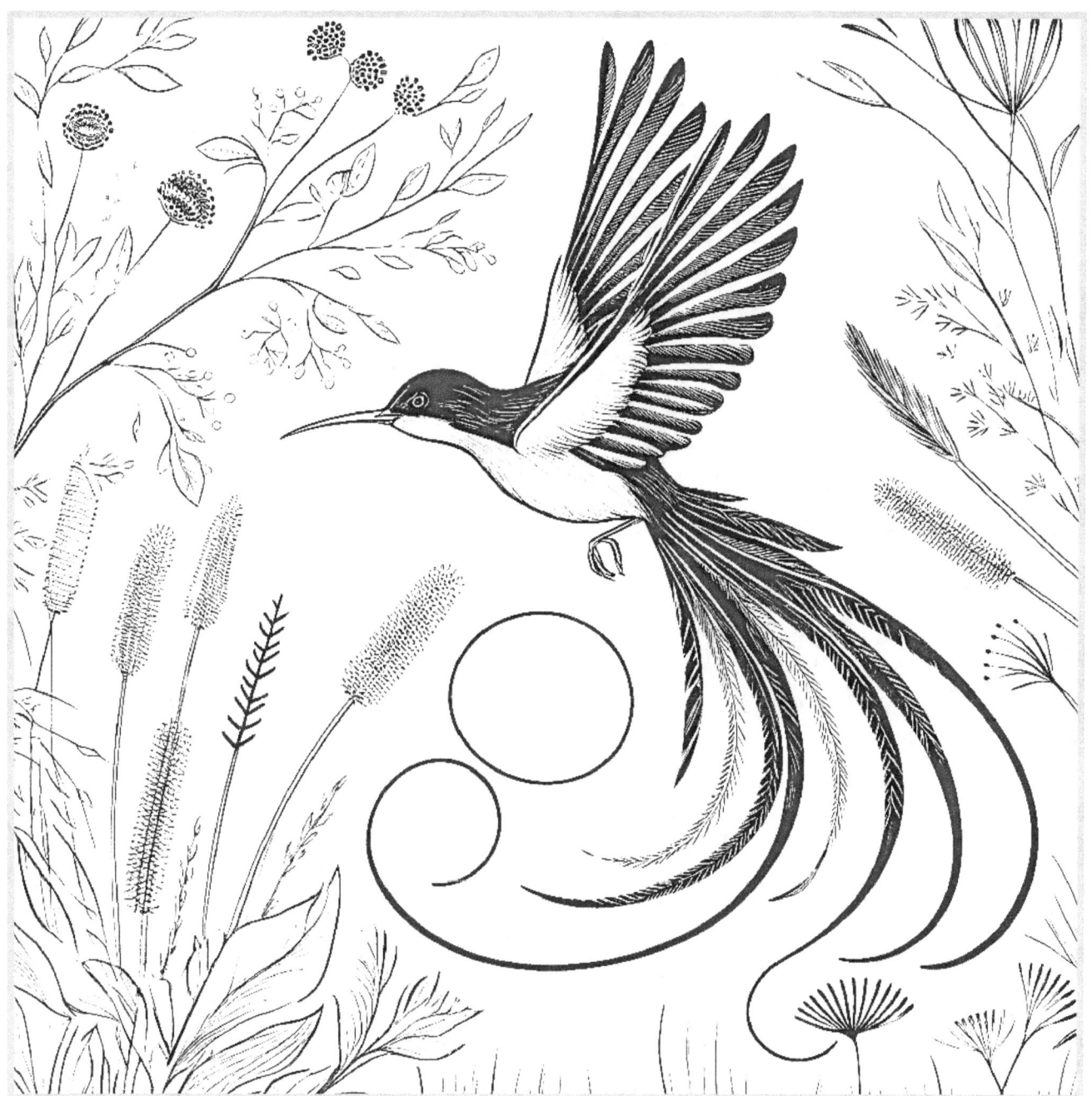

Pheasant

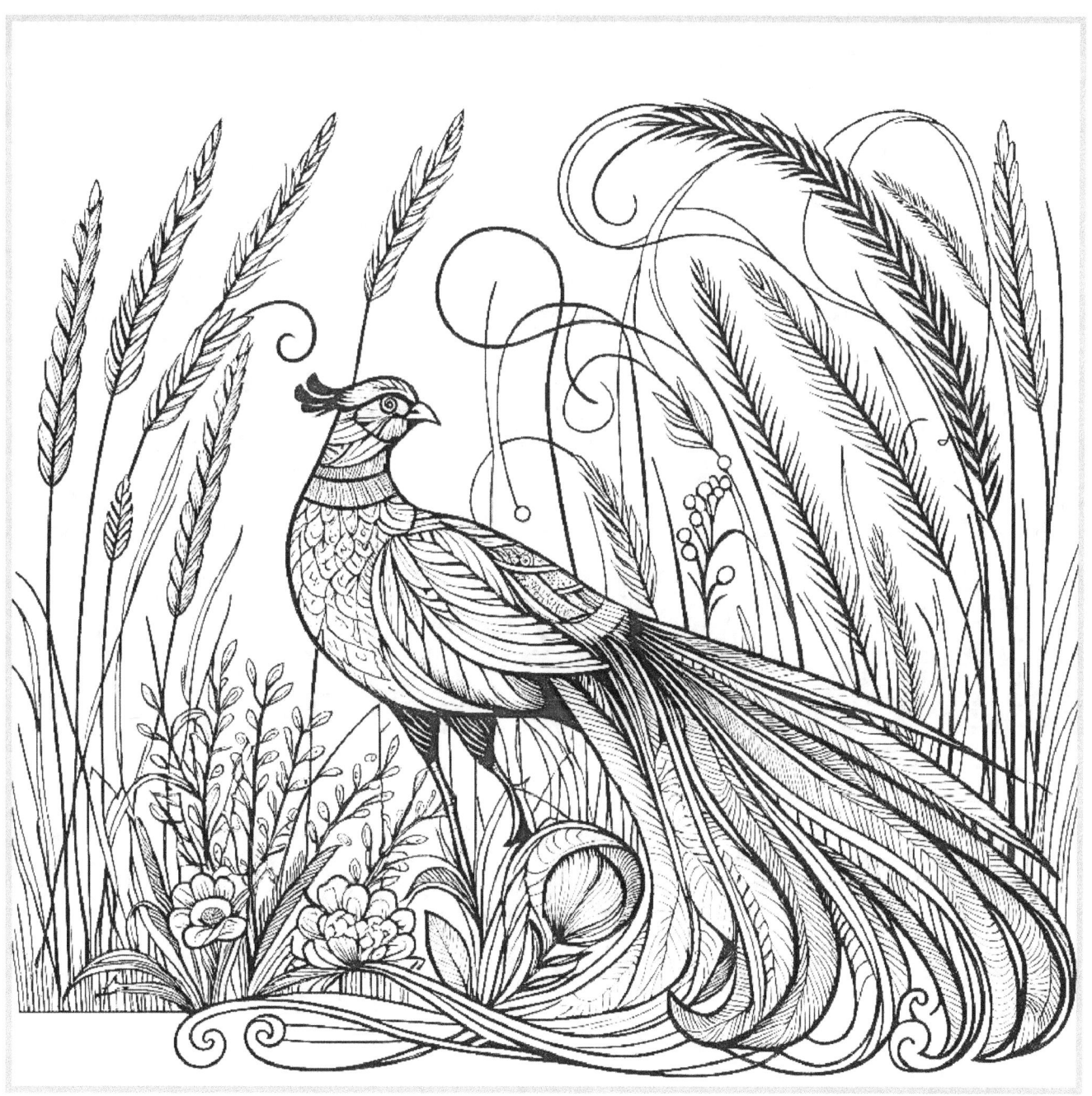

Scarlet Macaw

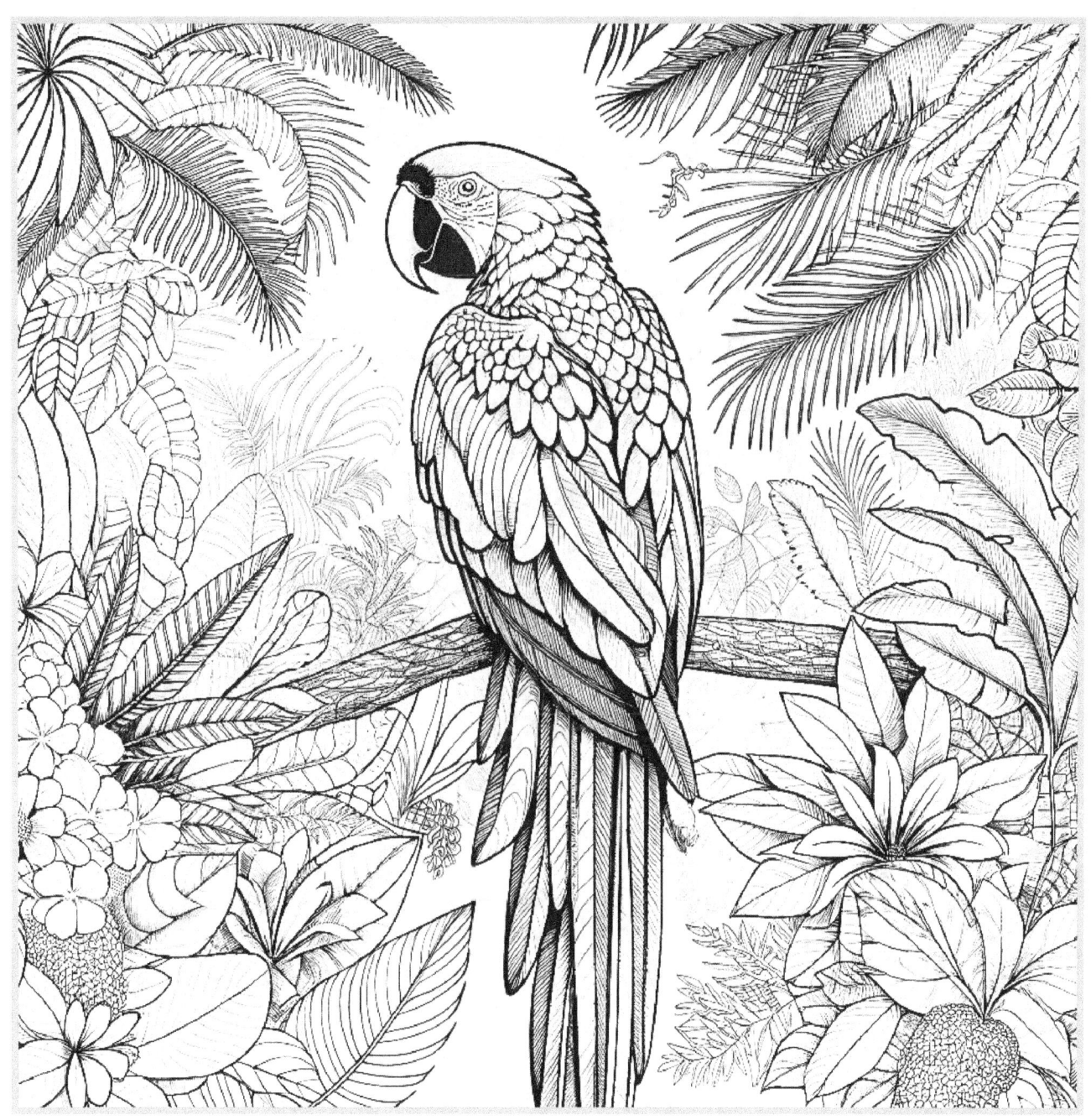

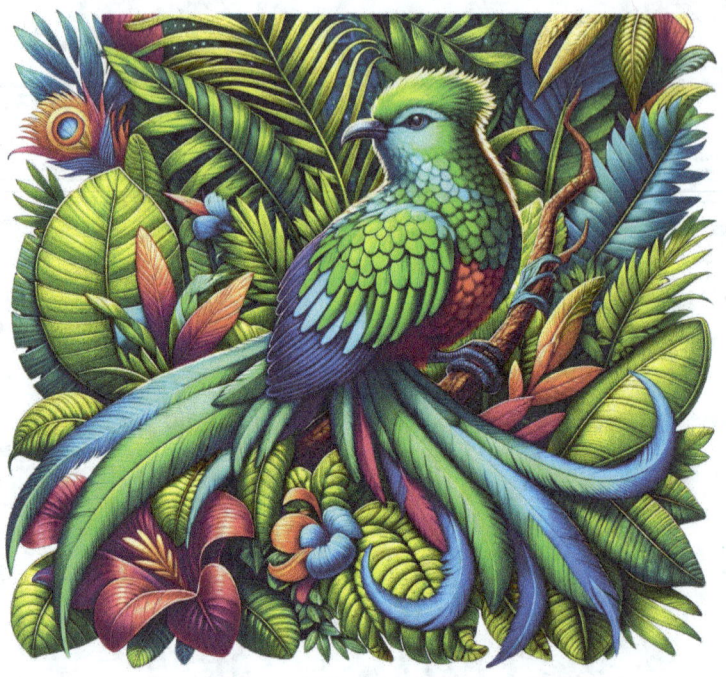

Jenifer Steller

Creative concepts developed in the organization and writing of this book are the creative and intellectual property of Jenifer J. Steller. All materials are commercially licensed.

www.ingramcontent.com/pod-product-compliance
Lightning Source LLC
Chambersburg PA
CBHW062227220526
45471CB00009B/3384